❝Germana Rovinelli's book "We Do Recover" represents her recovery from her childhood and upbringing that few of us could recover from. It is not just a narrative but more importantly, a teaching story without her trying to be a teacher. Nevertheless, it is letting us know that this is what she did to get hold of her life and grow into the beautiful human being she is. Step by step without pretense, she just does it. In effect she's letting us know "If I can do it, so can you."❞

—*Fatha K. Taylor, Councellor / Teacher / Mentor*

❝Through her trials and tribulations—Germana is able to offer others who may have experienced similar circumstances, the ability to dream and follow your dreams regardless of how damaged or flawed they may feel deep down inside. It offers the reader hope, regardless of the trauma—that there is hope, and to believe that change is always possible, and that "We Do Recover". Thank you for sharing your story. Much love and respect.❞

—*Valerie Kuilboer*

❝This book is baout the lineage that resulted in a resilient spirit who sought recovery. Not just recovery from substances, but also all the family rules, shame and trauma that addiction thrives in. It is a tribute to the hard work, perseverance and sheer determination and desperation it takes to stay clean and heal from intergenerational trauma, no matter how hard, painful and at times hopeless it feels.❞

—*Jade Seabrook*

 FriesenPress

Suite 300 - 990 Fort St
Victoria, BC, V8V 3K2
Canada

www.friesenpress.com

Copyright © 2021 by Germana Rovinelli
First Edition — 2021

Edited by Goody Niosi

Property of G H & W S inc

All rights reserved.

No part of this publication may be reproduced in any form, or by any means, electronic or mechanical, including photocopying, recording, or any information browsing, storage, or retrieval system, without permission in writing from FriesenPress.

ISBN
978-1-5255-8734-4 (Hardcover)
978-1-5255-8733-7 (Paperback)
978-1-5255-8735-1 (eBook)

1. BIOGRAPHY & AUTOBIOGRAPHY, PERSONAL MEMOIRS

Distributed to the trade by The Ingram Book Company

WE DO RECOVER

BY GERMANA ROVINELLI
Who DID Recover.

This book is dedicated to all the recovery communities

TABLE OF CONTENTS

Foreword	1
Chapter 1	3
Chapter 2	17
Chapter 3	35
Chapter 4	55
Chapter 5	73
Chapter 6	87
Chapter 7	99
Chapter 8	109
Chapter 9	117
Chapter 10	135
Chapter 11	141
Chapter 12	155
Afterword	161
Thank You	167
Recovery Resources	187
About the Author	193

FOREWORD

A butcher who hung himself in the kitchen like a slab of meat; a stream of young men, who raped me, abused me, assaulted me, and used me; a father who rejected me, abandoned me, and almost killed me; a road of self-destruction, drugs, and alcohol that led me to the brink of annihilation.

This was my history—but not my end.

I developed into a Canadian champion bodybuilder and winner of more than a dozen trophies. I operate Able Body Consulting as a mind/body coach and trainer. I am a certified hypnotherapist, a Jazzercise instructor, and a certified neurolinguistic-programming practitioner. I teach others how to navigate through adversity and lead a life centred on fulfillment.

This is my story: how I overcame an horrific childhood, survived a dysfunctional family, and forged a way to sobriety.

Regardless of the challenges you face, I hope that what you find in these pages helps add a chapter to your story: recovery and new beginnings.

I was a single mother, mired in pain and disappointments. My past smothered me in shame and self-hatred. But I found inspiration. An ember of promise still burning within me became a flame, ignited by world-class teachers, including masters in martial arts, hypnotherapy practitioners, and senior yoga instructors.

Through daily practice and an intense desire to create a fulfilling future, I gathered resources and tools that I want to share with you.

I learned that I am worthy of acceptance and love.

So are you.

People can heal. They can live the life they envision. Everyone is worth saving, and the tools to make peace with yourself and your past are available. I hope this book helps you on this path to healing—to becoming the whole human being you know exists within.

We do recover.

CHAPTER 1

I didn't stand a chance.

Neither did my parents and nor did theirs. But chance or no chance, these are the people who gave birth to me, and these are the people I survived. And that's the key—I survived.

I bore my father's beatings, betrayals, disparagements, and horrific abuse. I lived through his repeated attempts at drowning me. I came close to the edge of death many times. Did he care that his acts threatened my life—damaged me to a point where I thought myself irreparable? Had he hated me? I don't know, but he didn't know how to love me; of that, I am sure. I had to beg for love—from him, from my mother, and then from every man I met until I got help. I would probably have been a doctor or a lawyer or a veterinarian if I'd had a loving foundation. If my father had been there for me, I would have been a different person.

But I'm not. Based on an improbable history, I'm me. I carry with me a long train of boxcars filled with the pain and trauma of my parents and the generations preceding them. Sometimes the train feels like it stretches from here to Siberia.

My mother, Monika, is in one of those boxcars, born in Dresden, Germany in 1939—in the area that became

East Germany after the war. She was the oldest of nine children. Her father, Karl, was a Nazi soldier. Her mother, Charlotte, looked after the house and children. They were poor, but they owned a farm and grew most of their own food.

Monika grew up with the sounds of bombs exploding around her day and night, her belly hungry, her body cold, and haunted by the stench of death and the sight of rotting bodies as commonplace as dandelions in a field.

She told me once about the vast increase in the owl population because so many rats and mice fed on the corpses that were piled in ditches, roads, and laneways.

And yet, that was only part of her misery. Her father was a pedophile. When her mother pleaded with the church for help, the priest told her that if she performed better as a wife, her husband wouldn't sexually assault his children.

At 18, Monika escaped East Germany before the erection of the infamous wall; it was not an escape from the Russians but from her own family. She arrived in Dusseldorf and soon after married a butcher. I imagine that for her it seemed a good bargain: I give you my body, you give me the stability of a job and food on the table.

Still, she was a beautiful young woman, but one with little life experience. She was irresistibly drawn to the Friday night dances at the local hall, and when her butcher didn't go with her, she went alone. She met men there—many men. One night she danced with an Italian named Piero Rovinelli—the man who became my father.

Piero was born to a beggar couple in Italy soon after the war. His mother was blind, and he referred to his father as "the town loser" who brought his young son with him when he did his street rounds, looking for handouts from the Allied soldiers. Piero's father was eventually committed to a mental institution, leaving his mother to cope with five children. She brought the three oldest, including Piero, to an orphanage, taking the youngest with her because the smaller ones were better at eliciting sympathy and convincing people to part with their meagre liras.

"I'll come back for you," she said. She never did.

Piero must have been devastated. He peed his bed until he was 13 years old, but instead of being treated with empathy by the nuns, they shamed him by hanging his stained mattress out the window. And so he became a loner.

He concluded that the only way to escape was through education, and he proved himself adept at academics. Before he left the orphanage, he had taught himself to speak seven languages. His second love was dancing.

And so he met my mother at a Friday night dance in Dusseldorf. The tale she tells of the tragedy that followed is that the butcher saw them dancing, rushed home in grief, and hung himself in the kitchen. I believe he caught them having sex and hanged himself, not only from grief but also a desire for revenge. Several hours later, that's how Monika found him—dangling like one of his sides of beef from a hook. Horrified, she ran back to Piero for comfort—for anything to erase that sight.

My father believed that the man's death was his fault, and now Monika was a widow with no means of support. They married, with Piero replacing the butcher out of guilt, self-hatred, and duty, but not love.

They decided to have children, at least Monika did: first a boy and then, a year later, a girl. That girl was me.

My sense was that my father hadn't wanted children because after our births, everything changed. His wife's world no longer revolved around him. He became verbally and physically abusive to my mother and to the babies. Unprovoked beatings were a normal part of our lives.

In 1968, when I was two years old, my parents escaped their endless misery and moved to Canada. In Montreal, they planned to start over and give themselves and their children a better life. Piero had trained as a machinist—that job would pay well, he reasoned. But within weeks of landing in this new country, he found an apartment in Oak Bay in Victoria, British Columbia, and we moved across the country.

I wasn't aware of all his issues, but even at that age, I could see that he wasn't well. He often stumbled when he walked; he dropped things and then lost some of his sight. He also became meaner.

Soon after we settled in Oak Bay, my father studied to become a schoolteacher. He completed his training and received his certificate, but two weeks after entering a classroom for the first time, the school board fired him. He didn't only lose his job; he was also banned from the education system because he treated his students like he did his own children: screaming, yelling, slapping, and threatening them. I suspect that he was acting out what he had learned at the orphanage or perhaps at his church, or he was re-enacting his own childhood. But he was without work and unable to earn a living.

My mother filed for divorce, but he continued to live in the house, where he beat her, forcing us to watch as we sat around the kitchen table. If we cried, he would attempt to strangle us or drown us in the kitchen sink. If we kept crying, he whipped us and if that didn't work he would throw us in the closet with the lights off. Our house was a war zone. I never knew from day to day and sometimes from minute to minute if I was in trouble for something I had either done or failed to do.

I often felt responsible for my mother's suffering. She would work hard for a while but would eventually break down, sobbing and drinking. If we showed sadness, anger, or fear, she would beat us, and if we didn't stop crying from the beatings, both she and my father would run water in the sink and partially drown us to make us stop.

I numbed myself.

I tried to go unnoticed. I ran and hid. I didn't talk to people. Being seen or recognized terrified me. Mostly, I knew something was wrong with me. It was my fault.

There was one small light in my dark nightmare. We lived two blocks from Sealand and the Oak Bay Rose Garden on Newport Avenue, and that's where I connected with life. I went to the park every chance I got. I climbed trees and skipped rocks into the ocean.

At school I was shy and surprised, even startled, that my teachers didn't hurt me because I thought that was part of education, even part of life. My father, who was committed to making us learn, would sit us down at the table with an encyclopaedia and cue cards and he would drill us with facts far beyond our ages. If I couldn't repeat what he wanted me to, he would beat me—and then the drowning, and then being shaken like a rag doll. I knew then that nothing I did would ever be good enough.

He was publicly abusive. Strangers would stop in the street and attempt to intervene. He would trip us, slap us, and yell at us. People would try to take us away from him. They would say, "You can't do that to these children."

He would say, "I can do anything I want. I'm their father. Ask them—they will tell you."

And we would admit, "He's our father."

These kind, caring strangers, in absolute horror, would hand us back to him, and the ridicule and beatings would continue. We have memories of having our heads jammed down a toilet because we failed to finish our breakfast. My brother remembers being held underwater in the bathtub for crying.

My mother's divorce filing came through when I was five. If my memory is accurate, I think my father was physically removed from the premises. That was one of the happiest days we can recall.

I entered grade one. My mother worked as a seamstress and part-time as a housekeeper. Sometimes she brought me with her. I remember going to a wealthy woman's house and saying to my mother, "She's smiling, but she's not happy."

"You're right," Mom said. "She's not happy."

But neither was she. Her affairs with married men were an effort to fill a void—sex was the only contact she wanted with men—or perhaps the only contact she felt she deserved. I believe she was also re-enacting her childhood and the sexual abuse she had suffered.

I continued to find my joy, what little there was, at Sealand. I watched the killer whales—Haida and Shimo— and I would burrow into the rose garden and hide there and pretend I was safe. Piero was gone, but my mother sometimes flew into rages. We never knew when they were coming, but when they did, they terrified me. I'm sure she was a narcissist. I know that she was an alcoholic.

And then she passed her Power Squadron tests and got a 19-foot boat that she kept at the local marina. And she bought horses. We had always been around horses, and because my mother had grown up on a farm, horses were an important part of her life. She got me a Shetland pony named Chester and for her, a retired RCMP horse named Pancho. There was also a palomino called Panda Bear. She boarded them at the old Judges farm in Saanich with hundreds of acres bordering Thetis Lake. We'd go out there, find the horses, brush them, tack them up, and then ride them on all that land.

But nothing my mother did was straightforward. She was having an affair with the man who sold Chester to her, and he may have sold her the other horses too. Chester was fat and crazy mean. I would get on him and he would buck me off, bite me, and run away. Then I'd have to chase him down and get on him again. After I'd done that dozens of times, I told my mom, "I refuse to ride that horse again." So she started riding the pony while I rode the horse.

At school, I discovered a small talent for athletics. I was especially good at running, so I competed in track and won a place on the relay team. I made pom-poms out of newspapers and liked to sit in the stands, cheering for the school teams.

I was also good at stealing. Because we had nothing, I saw it as a necessity. I didn't have clothes, so I stole them. My mother didn't understand about school or my need to fit in. I asked her once to make Kraft Dinner because my friend's mom made it. My mother said it was garbage food, but she boiled the pasta and dropped it into a bowl. She poured milk over the top, emptied the packed of orange "cheese" over it, and topped that with a pat of butter. And that was the only time we had Kraft Dinner.

Our apartment on Newport Avenue was above Morgan's Store, and the owners allowed us to have a charge account. Mom was rarely there, so I ate a lot of junk food. I comforted myself with Ding Dongs, Twinkies, canned beans, and tinned ravioli. I was four when I started frying my own eggs, but mostly I stuffed myself with saturated fats and sugars and episodes of *Gilligan's Island*, *The Brady Bunch*, and *The Munsters*.

No one taught us proper hygiene like brushing our teeth, combing our hair, or washing our clothes. Once a teacher sent me home with a note requesting that I arrive at school with my hair combed, my teeth brushed, and fresh clothing. My mother read the note and whipped me. She didn't know it was her job to look after me; instead, she repeated the shame and abuse of her own childhood.

Food wasn't the only thing I used to stuff my feelings. My parents let us drink alcohol from the age of two, when they gave us booze to help us sleep. They thought it was cute when we got drunk. The rules were: don't think; don't talk; don't feel. Do as I say, not as I do. The underlying message was: you're bad; it's all your fault.

Above all else, I felt shame. I felt like I didn't exist. My only purpose was to look after and raise my mother. When I went to school and learned English, I would come home and teach my mother. My father spoke seven languages, but I refused to even speak German and I never have. Being bilingual meant being like my dad.

Whenever he came around, he hurt us. Hate was all I felt for him. I found a picture once of my father trying to hug me and there I was horrified, recoiling—trying to escape him. He revolted me.

I think my parents had my brother and I to heal the damage that had been done to them. We weren't born to be loved, protected, and nourished; we were born to look after them. I didn't have a sense of identity. Everything I did was based on trying not to get killed.

I was older when I realized that something strange was happening with my brother. He was into skateboarding and cool music and then, when he was about eight years old, he started stuttering. Nobody could fathom what was going on. Years later, when I was working through my own issues with sexual abuse, I found out that his best friend's older brother had groomed him and sexually abused him. Nobody noticed and my brother's life fell apart while we watched.

I was 11 when my mother moved us to Cobble Hill, where she got a job at a cedar furniture plant. We lived on the top floor of a beautiful house converted from an old barn. Gary Graham, the owner, his wife, Donna, and son, Billy, lived below us. My mother had had an affair with Gary, however briefly, and it didn't take long before Billy started assaulting me. My mother walked in on us one day. He was on top of me, tearing at my clothes. She grabbed my riding crop and started whipping me in front of him.

He was, after all, the landlord's son. While blood oozed down my back and I bit back the screams of pain, shame overpowered me. I was convinced the beating was because I had done something wrong. And Billy watched. He knew that no one would protect me. I had nowhere to run.

Billy gave me pot and, once stoned, he would fuck me.

Billy's mother was an alcoholic while mine was probably still having clandestine sex with his father.

At that time, my father got the odd idea that my mother needed a boyfriend, so he put an ad in the newspaper—and that's how Adam Balmer came into our lives. Adam operated several factories manufacturing clothes and handbags. He, his two sons, and his daughter became part of our lives in Cobble Hill, until he decided that we would live with him in Maple Ridge on the mainland, where my mother was going to help him in his factories.

We all moved to his big house, and I started grade eight in a posh city school where the students ranked each other based on beauty and style. I didn't fit in at all.

Adam's oldest son, Phillip, was a few years my senior and abused me daily. When I told my mother that Phillip was sexually assaulting me, she slapped me across the face. "You're lying," she said. "You just want attention."

At 14, I packed my bags and hitched a ride back to Vancouver Island, where I contacted Steven Eliot—a boy I had dated a couple of times. He let me stay in the family trailer at Lake Cowichan. His older brother Jerry found out, came to the trailer, burst into the bathroom while I was having a shower, and raped me. When Steven found out, he moved me to another brother's house, and he also came after me.

I don't remember how I escaped it all. Nowhere was safe. I got thrown into jail for shoplifting, and when they asked me why I had stolen a facecloth, I said, "Because I wanted to wash my face."

I was finally put into foster care near Mission on the mainland. The family had a big veal farm and put their foster kids to work, but they also treated us pretty well. Fran taught me how to bake, and we would spend time together in the kitchen, making cookies and muffins. Then they brought in another young man who was a sexual predator. By this time, I wasn't surprised when he came after me. This was my life. I ran away again, this time to my friend, Denise's house.

Denise's mother took me in because she collected welfare, and as a foster child, I was a source of income for her. She was a drug addict who had no qualms about giving us pot, LSD, and alcohol. She sold drugs too, so I thought I'd died and gone to heaven.

I got expelled from school. The final offence was changing an E to a B in my report card. I was told that I had one of two choices: leave or improve. I left.

Within two days I was working at Murray's Bakery, a European establishment in Maple Ridge Mall.

I loved the way it smelled when I walked in every morning: bread, cookies, and glazed donuts fresh from the oven and the fryer. I worked in the front of the bakery, always terrified of making a mistake, so I cut and bagged bread better than anyone they had ever hired. They marvelled at my work ethic, not knowing that I was motivated by the fear that I would be fired, discarded, and rejected just as I had been by my family. *You're not good enough* was the theme that played in my mind all day every day.

All my hard work was earning me $3.65 an hour.

Still, I loved the job. I knew my role. The customers were happy. Everyone was happy. The bakery was clean and I enjoyed watching the way my boss, Eva, decorated her gorgeous cakes. She was an outstanding artist. She was also cheerful and kind. I was allowed to eat as much as I wanted, but after two weeks of gorging, I was no longer tempted by all the rich treats. I happily packed them for the customers knowing that they tasted great but would likely settle under their skin as fat for a lot longer than they realized.

I was dating Ricki, my foster mother's oldest son who was in his twenties and a psychopath, but he had a flashy car and the lifestyle I wanted: drinking, smoking pot, concerts—and sex. That's how I paid my way. I became an efficient alcoholic. I could drink an entire bottle of tequila on my own.

Ricki had been abandoned by his mother and lived with his grandparents, believing they were his biological parents. His younger brother, Earl, had been told the same lie. They drank and partied and had a great hate for society and the world in general. When they discovered that the woman who was my foster mother was their real mother, they fell apart.

She was an addict whose habit had taken control of her life—and her sons hated her for it. Her husband, Bob, was a kind, responsible man, yet she had numerous affairs. One day, he ended the marriage.

When I met Ricki at age 14, he chose me because I was young and "tighter" than the other girls he'd had sex with. In fact, I was a child, and Ricki was 23 years old.

No one stopped him, certainly not my foster mother, probably because of the secrets she kept from him. I had no objections. The situation was ideal, but then the cycle of abuse began. It started with the attraction, then the overwhelming feeling of love. Then he began to criticize my body. I became his property and his validation. Then he abused me and had sex with other people, blaming me all the while. Then he told me I was crazy when I presented him with evidence of his cheating.

After that, the beatings began.

If I can't have you, no one can have you. I'll kill you if you leave me.

We were together for two years. By the time I was 16, I was an addict.

In the beginning, he treated me well; then, he exposed me to drinking binges and parties. He was unfaithful. When he contracted an STD, he blamed me. Lucky for me, when I got tested, my results came back clean. And still, Ricki continued to have sex with other women, often being set up by Doug Cote, a mutual friend.

Once I found a friend's ring and underwear in Ricki's bed. That was when I ended the relationship. That's also when the stalking began. Like my father, Ricki was a sociopath.

CHAPTER 2

I moved back in with my mother soon after Alan Balmer abandoned her, leaving her with thousands of dollars of bills to pay off while earning minimum wage. She rented a big old farmhouse on Dewdney Trunk Road, where she kept horses, chickens, and cats, and spent most of her time crying, drinking wine, and working two front-line jobs: driving twelve-hour taxi shifts and working the cash register at a convenience store. To help with finances, the house had its share of sublet tenants.

A picture of the Virgin Mary hung on her taxicab meter that she prayed to, to keep her safe. I wonder if she felt like a child in a war zone again, when her own mother had put pictures of the angels Michael and Raphael over her bed. While her mother had prayed to keep her daughter safe from soldiers and bombs, her husband had sexually assaulted her child.

History repeating itself.

I continued to work at the bakery and brought some of those skills home. I had also made new friends. One renter who lived with us introduced me to a van club, where I met a man I liked a lot.

But Ricki, my old psychopath lover, had no intention of letting me go. My new boyfriend and I were sleeping in his van one night, parked in our driveway, when Ricki drove by, saw the van, broke into it, and beat the man badly.

"She's mine," he told him.

I never saw my beautiful, rock-star-handsome friend again.

I was sure it was my fault: my fault that Ricki had hurt this man; my fault that I had lost him; my fault that I was in desperate emotional pain again.

History repeated itself less than a year later when I ran into Wade, a friend from Vancouver Island. We started seeing each other, and I let him stay with me in my room. Again, in the middle of the night, Ricki burst in and beat Wade until his face was unrecognizable.

"You're mine!" he yelled at me.

I never saw Wade again, but Ricki kept stalking me.

I kept searching for peace and security and found a measure of it at the local arcade where I hung out with the Hany gang. We were unwanted teenagers with nothing to look forward to but being with each other and getting high. Groups kept me safe, or so I thought. But Ricki had a way of knowing when and where to find me.

One night, after an evening with the gang, I walked from the arcade to the downtown park in Maple Ridge, feeling calm and happy. Out of nowhere, Ricki pulled up, flying out of his car towards me. Before I could think or react, he beat me, calling me a whore, saying that if he couldn't have me, no one could. I had no way to protect myself, and I remember little, although I believe bystanders prevented him from dragging me into his car.

And then, just like that, I never saw Ricki again. Maybe he found another target, or he moved away or died. But the damage he inflicted was horrific, and proved to be a precursor to the pain and abuse to come.

My girlfriend at the time was a pretty blonde named Laura. We would keep each other company, which usually meant going out drinking and drugging and looking for fun. One day, on a whim, we decided to hitchhike to Vancouver.

An older man in his late twenties, Doug Urquhart, gave us a ride. Doug was an upscale drug dealer on his way to pick up an ounce of pure cocaine. He asked if we wanted to come party with him. We said yes and went to his mansion in Mission, where we slept with him.

He selected me to be his girlfriend. He bought me a car and paid for driving lessons. I felt rescued, valued, and important: feelings I had never experienced with my family—a rush more potent than any drug. And he had good drugs—very good drugs, including cocaine. I revelled in having something so exotic and expensive so readily available to me. When he stopped giving it to me, I would wait until he was gone and stand in the basement and ask myself. "If I was hiding the stash from me, were would I put it?" Within minutes, sometimes seconds, I would find it, take a spoonful out, and put some cut or sugar in it, shake it, and put it back.

Along with feeding my addiction, I was also fuelling my denial and shame. I lost 25 pounds and my bones stuck out, but I convinced myself that I looked beautiful. Within six months, I destroyed my car. Doug dumped me after that, taking me back to my mother's house and discarding me like a used pair of shoes.

My mother was bitter. On my sixteenth birthday, she gave me a used ice cream scoop and a second-hand mug with the letters DB on it, informing me that DB stood for "dumb bitch." How to describe how that felt: like a massive hole had been blown through my centre.

I drank harder than ever—anything to numb the pain of being alive without support, love, or guidance. I had always felt like a third-rate person; now, my mother had confirmed and cemented that into my soul.

I was 16, addicted to cocaine, with no purpose in life other than being high or loaded or looking for someone to rescue or fix me. I had become accustomed to having free access to cocaine, and being back home with my mother—a home that was cold and unloving—was doubly traumatizing. My solace was hanging out with other people my age, living mostly on the street, and partying.

I don't recall the exact day I met Mark Funk, a German whose father had abandoned his family. Mark lived with his mother, who had tried to commit suicide in the bathroom by slicing open her wrists and the veins behind her knees. As a result, she had been lobotomized and lived with her children in a near-vegetative state.

The kids survived in their Maple Ridge house by stealing, dumpster diving, and dealing drugs. Mark and I gravitated towards each other because we understood our commonalities and failings. He was introverted and incapable of looking after himself, including the basics of personal hygiene.

I left my mother's house and moved in with him, making him my project, one that lasted seven years—and I suppose I became his. I never had to ask for money. There was food in the house, and I had a place to sleep. Still, it was a dysfunctional home that resembled a commune where his brother and girlfriend lived with us, and another brother and his wife shacked up in another house on the property.

The brothers had gone to great lengths to protect their venture, turning the house more into a fortress prepared for war than a place where people lived. They knew that the police were always gearing up for a drug bust. They bought derelict Cadillacs to barricade the house. Anyone coming up the driveway had to run an intricate old-car obstacle course. Tripwires crossed the windows; the door swung out rather than in, and reinforced exterior and interior walls made entry difficult. If the police ever made it inside, a big bucket of water stood ready by the toilet to flush the drugs.

One of Mark's brothers was smart enough to go to law school, funding his education by dealing drugs. But the minute he got his law degree and passed the bar, the police busted him and they never allowed him to practice. He went into a deep rage against society—maybe against everything.

I saw him more than once weighing out the pot he was selling while he was high on some medication. There he was: three pounds of pot by one side and a buyer on his other, and he would freeze and fall asleep standing up. We'd have to finish the deal and see the guy out.

The family's model was make money, fuck the system, and blame everyone else.

Still, to me, Mark was more like a brother than a lover. I was not attracted to him, and I avoided sexual intimacy as much as possible. But Mark had other ideas and, reluctantly, I gave him the pleasure he wanted because he provided the money, even for a new intense interest: martial arts.

Cathy, the girlfriend of Mark's would-be lawyer brother—who was also sleeping with another of Mark's brothers—introduced Mark and I to a karate dojo. Mark helped me to pay for these new joys in my life while simultaneously telling me I was too stupid to make anything of myself.

As soon as I met with the karate instructor and listened to him, I knew Mark had likely found himself a new client. Once home, I told Mark, "Sensei is on cocaine. He's completely wired." And soon after training began, Sensei asked if he could buy cocaine from us.

I had no respect for the man, but the discipline of karate taught me how to be a better person; it showed me how to take my anger and frustration and externalize it instead of turning it inward on myself. Karate taught me to speak up and to ask for what I needed and wanted. It also met my need for a place to belong.

Ironically, that was how my fitness career began. It felt natural to gravitate towards that. When I was a child, the only time I felt safe was when I was outside running or playing or moving my body. I needed the physical outlet to balance the emotional stress I lived with every day. I was anxious, nervous, and afraid all the time.

I also had an image issue. Going to a fitness class gave me a physical challenge; at the end of the session, I invariably felt better about myself. I was so afraid of becoming an overweight teenager. That fear played low-key background music in my life; I was afraid of being rejected. I thought I had no value—not that I could have articulated that thought. All I knew was that I was driven to exercise.

So I went to classes. I had a beautiful instructor, Maggie Britten, who looked like Oprah Winfrey with blond hair and blue eyes. She was good and I worshipped her. She wore headbands, makeup, and leg warmers: a one-woman glamour show. And there I was, wanting to fit in—looking for a family, something bigger than myself that I could be part of—a place where I belonged. Sometimes I would go to classes twice a day.

Maggie impressed me with how she looked: she was in such incredible shape and she was in her thirties. I was 16—this woman had to be doing something right.

One day, as the class was wrapping up, I told her how fabulous she was, and she said, "Anyone can do this. Anyone can become an instructor."
What?

And my next thought: *I've been coming all this time—I may as well get paid.* So I went to the YMCA in Vancouver, where I enrolled in my first instructor course. Within six months, I was looking for a place to teach, but no one wanted to take me on; the clubs were afraid of liability. I finally approached a small club and said, "I will teach for a month for free—as many classes as you want." I needed those hours to get certified.

I had no mentoring. But I'd stopped doing drugs, at least for a while, and I put in my hours and got certified. Then I went to Maggie and told her I was ready to teach.

She disagreed. She didn't say why, but I was convinced that I wasn't the right kind of girl for her. I had a tattoo, and I wasn't a tiny blonde with blue eyes and a narrow waist. I didn't look the part.

Still, she introduced me to a friend who owned an aerobic dance studio and who was thrilled with my skill set.

I taught a lot of fitness classes; it was my new addiction. People listened to what I had to say, and they respected me—that was heady. I was soon teaching up to 18 classes a week in a variety of locations. When I wasn't teaching, I was driving from one studio to another. As a bonus, I was being paid well.

I was so wrapped up in my new passion that I failed to recognize that I was burning out. I just kept going until I fell off a cliff. I had car accidents—so many that the insurance company became suspicious that I was operating a scam. And I was so tired that I started using again. However, the lawyer who was working on my cases assured me that sooner or later I was going to receive a substantial payout. What would I do when that happened? I had no experience managing money. The people I lived with were on drugs; they were paranoid, neurotic, lying, thieving, and borderline insane.

Mark and I got our black belts together. To celebrate, he insisted that I learn to ride a motorcycle. We were so bad, riding around on his Harley Chopper, drugged out of our minds. We'd be awake on drugs for three days and then crash at six in the morning.

Getting high, crashing vehicles, and losing men became a theme. One day, I was driving Mark's favourite truck, slammed it into a telephone pole and destroyed it. He was devastated, and I believe that one of the reasons I stayed with him so long was because I felt guilty about the truck. I didn't love him. I cried when he wanted to have sex with me.

My instability became more pronounced when I developed a severe eating disorder. I hated myself and my body. I wanted to be thin and healthy, so I ate wholesome foods; I cooked and baked and exercised. I became a vegetarian. I forced myself onto diets but didn't know what I was doing. All the anxiety, crash dieting, and fear led me to sleepwalking in the middle of the night, directly to the refrigerator, and devouring the food that belonged to the others in the house. Cathy worked at Essendale, the mental institution in New Westminster, and she would get up at four a.m., reach for the lunch she'd made the night before, and find nothing.

I'd eat and go back to sleep and wake up in the morning to food in the bed and food in my mouth and a full stomach. I gained about 40 pounds. I thought that I was doing this unconsciously so that Mark would leave me alone. Years later, I learned that sleep eating is linked to sexual abuse and to not having a voice.

I eventually broke that pattern, but not wisely—drugs fuelled my new diet. I received a significant amount of money from my accident settlements. I could have retired on it and been comfortable for the rest of my life. Instead, I put it in the bank and started taking it out: $500 one day, $750 another day. Within six months, I'd spent it all on drugs. I was no longer teaching. I was doing nothing but drugs.

I didn't want to face my life or myself. I was going to die anyway, so I might as well go with drugs. I overdosed twice. I remember being out of my body and going to another place where there were beings. Maybe angels? Guides? They talked to me, told me I had to go back. Twice. I had grand mal seizures and convinced myself that I had so much brain damage there was nothing left worth saving.

Mark was also doing a lot of drugs and becoming crazier. One day, his brothers came into our room, put a gun to my head, and said, "You're leaving." I loaded up my car—my 1964 SS Impala—and drove to Vancouver Island with my dog, Booboo. With nowhere else to go, I went to my mom, who now lived with her partner near Sooke.

I remember that time as the darkest of my life. I had my car, my dog, and my drugs. I was smoking three packs of cigarettes a day. I'd just arrived on the island when I drove to downtown Victoria where I met an older man: a biker who professed to be a Wiccan high priest. He showered me with attention, told me he knew my soul—and I was desperate, hungry for exactly what he was dishing up.

I married him within weeks, and in an instant, it all came crashing down. He was a criminal and a psychopath. In effect, I had married my father. Two weeks after our wedding, he was arrested and thrown into jail. So I got a job as a short-order cook at Mom's Café in Sooke. That's where I met Lisa, who also worked as a cook and was a recovering heroin addict who had been clean for a year.

I regularly drove to the Wilkinson Road jail to visit my husband. And we had lengthy telephone conversations—all for the sake of entertaining him. While he was incarcerated, I had a brief fling. When my husband got out of jail, I made the mistake of telling him. In a rage, he beat me senseless; my blood splattered on every wall. He screamed and screamed and punched me in the face over and over and over.

He would have killed me. My face was mashed. I don't remember how we got back to my mother's house. I remember flashes of his giant Bowie knife. Lisa had told me to get it away from him because he would kill me with it, and here he was with it in his hand, sitting me down on the couch—and throwing it. Over and over, I heard it thunk into the wall beside my head. Then he walked over, pulled it out, and threw it again, all the while yelling, "You're a slut! You're a whore!"

I agreed with him. "Yes, I'm horrible. Yes, I'm a whore." I would have agreed to anything just to stay alive. That day he was ready to decapitate me.

He finally left and went to the shack where we lived. I stumbled back, got Booboo, and staggered back to my mom's house, where I fell asleep in her bed. He came back for me, burst into the house, and rushed to the bedroom. "Over my dead body," my mom said, barring his way. But she wouldn't always be there, and it would only be a matter of time before he killed me. So I called the police and pressed charges.

Weeks later, after I'd healed and arrived in court, the police officers who had come to the house didn't recognize me. Who was this pretty girl? My physical healing took time; I'm not sure if I ever fully healed emotionally. Looking back, I believe he might have murdered his first wife because he'd used her as a threat. "Go against me and I'll show you what happened to my wife and two children."

The court sentenced him to two-plus years for battery and assault. But even behind bars, he tried to contact me until I had his phone privileges revoked. Yet somehow, even from jail, he was able to get to me. I had taken the jewellery that Mark had made for me and placed it in a sealed envelope in my lawyer's office for safekeeping. I don't know how, but he got someone to get to the secretary and take the most expensive pieces out. When I finally retrieved the envelope, those pieces had vanished.

With my husband in jail, I took stock of my life. I was sick; if I didn't stop using drugs, I would die. I asked Lisa to help me. She introduced me to Narcotics Anonymous in Sooke; it was what I wanted, but I wasn't ready to give up alcohol and drugs. I pretended I was clean, but I wasn't.

And then I ran into someone who had cocaine, my drug of choice. I stole money to pay for it. I was still working at Mom's Café, and I had started teaching fitness classes again at the hall across the street. But I was using and falling deeper and deeper into a black hole. I remember talking to a guy about how damaged and broken I was—about wanting more and it was never enough. When I didn't have enough money, I stole drugs and there was a rule about that—you get killed for stealing someone else's drugs.

And that was it—when I saw that the last shreds of my integrity had disappeared, I was ready to stop using. The date was February 21, 1990. I still had a bit of money from another accident settlement, so I left my mother's house and rented a room in Victoria, where I started going to recovery meetings. But all I was capable of was tears. I would sit in those meetings and cry and cry and cry. My life was over. I didn't know how to function. I felt stupid and worthless—a piece of trash.

I didn't know there were options for me. All I knew was that people like me were earmarked for death. We were homeless, useless, the sewer of the community. When people encountered us, they looked the other way.

But here I was in meetings, and people were talking about recovery—very little of that entered my consciousness. I believe I suffered from PTSD: I had scrambled and suppressed my emotions to survive a dystopian life, and I didn't know how to function in the world at large. I was an insect. I had no self-esteem. Everything frightened me. I didn't know how to protect myself from men. In relationships, I gave up and let them use me because I didn't know how to say no or how to mean no. I had sex with people I didn't know; one was Ron, an older man who told me he was sterile and didn't need a condom. I had sex with him only once—but that one time changed my life.

I met Arno at the meetings, a young German man who had been clean for a year. We had two things in common: we liked ZZ Top and we smoked. But he'd been drug-free for a year, and in my eyes, that made him some kind of god. If I hooked up with this guy, I wasn't going to die, so we began a relationship of sorts.

He was a fisherman—and me? I was crazy and broken. I begged for admission into a treatment facility, and to my shock, a miracle happened: a place opened up at the Victoria Life Enrichment Society (VLES). But my defences went up immediately: there were men here! I felt unsafe. Meanwhile, my breasts were swelling and tender. I was pregnant.

I told Arno. "It's not your child." I knew whose it was—the sterile Ron.

Arno said he didn't care. He was willing to be the child's father; he wanted me in his life. I was relieved that he wasn't ending our relationship because I wasn't brave enough to have an abortion. For me, it was simple: this was God's will; it was my next chapter.

But I was also pretty angry. I had sex with the lying Ron once—once! And I was having his baby. I found him and told him. "Well, then," he said. "We're going to get married."

I stared him down. "If you lied to me about being sterile, what else will you lie about? I don't trust you as far as I can throw you. You're a lying sack of shit. Get away from me. You abused my trust, and now I'm stuck being a mother with no father."

He threatened me, saying he would have me declared an unfit mother. "I'll have that baby taken away from you."

Another psychopath in my life: another abusive man trying to control me. He started stalking me. I'd look out the window of my room, and he would be there. I'd go to a meeting, and he was there. I was being hunted.

During that time, I went to a Narcotics Anonymous convention in Coquitlam. One of the speakers shared a story, and I cried and cried. It was all I could do. When I was asked to share what I was feeling, I said, "I didn't make mistakes. I am a mistake."

I was in the deepest imaginable pit of shame.

Back on Vancouver Island, with Ron still stalking me, I packed up my car and drove to Cassidy, south of Nanaimo, where Arno had a trailer in the Cassidy Trailer Park. Arno often went to work for months at a time, so I was alone. But even when he was there, he was clean, and I knew that if I stayed with him, I was not going to die. He was my survival.

With pregnancy, my body changed. I went to the Building Better Babies program and attended ADAPT, a program for people who wanted to stay clean. My counsellor, Renee Robson, was there to support me. I often sat in the ADAPT library, watching John Bradshaw videos as he talked about families and how it should be, and I remember looking at Renee, saying, "Please get me into treatment. I don't want to hurt my baby. I'm scared because I don't know how to love. I've never been loved. Please. Once the baby's here, it's too late."

She did everything she could for me. I was one year clean and almost nine months pregnant, and I got into Maya House for chemically dependent women.

That day was the day that saved me. That was the beginning of finding out who I am and of discovering what happened to me. I had forced myself to protect my mother rather than acknowledge that she had allowed me to be repetitively sexually abused, that she had never stood up for me.

At Maya House, I examined my entire history—every person I had slept with, all the way back to the very first one—and I shared that with the other women.

I went back and back all the way back to when I was 11, and the therapist said, "You were raped, and it was not your fault."

"No," I said. "I was a slut. I'm a whore."

She said, "No. You could lie on the floor screaming, 'Fuck me! Fuck me!' and if someone touched you, you would be raped because you're too young to know what you are giving up or what it meant."

"No," I said.

"Germana," she said. "Say this: 'I was raped and it wasn't my fault.'"

The group looked at me. "You were raped and it wasn't your fault," they said.

A hot flash of shame rushed through me like a tidal wave—and I fainted. I started shaking—a full-on seizure. I could not comprehend that I was not the one who was bad. Hadn't I always been bad?

My entire life—all of it—I had to look at it with entirely new eyes.

The therapist asked me to colour a large poster that I hung above my bed: "I was raped and it wasn't my fault."

Every day while I was in the facility, I had to look at that poster. And I had to acknowledge that I'd always felt dirty, that I had no value, that I felt like scum—and I would compensate by saying or doing anything just so that people would accept me.

The therapist encouraged me to report the rape. And I did. At that time, Worker's Compensation had a department dealing with injury and trauma, so they were involved as well as the police.

When I left the treatment centre, I moved in with Arno's family on their farm in Cedar. His mother and father welcomed me, believing the child I would give birth to any day was Arno's.

Konrad Arno Julian Rovinelli was born on May 10, 1991. It was a difficult delivery. The forceps may have caused some small brain damage, but he was a healthy eight-pound boy, and on his birth certificate, it said, "Father unknown."

CHAPTER 3

For the next weeks and months, I was content, and what an odd sensation that was. I hadn't experienced peace and joy, certainly not for any lengthy period. Mothering and nurturing Konrad filled me with love and responsibility, and the desire to be a good mother. I used cloth diapers; I breastfed him and had him sleep beside me, knowing he was safe when I could hear him breathing in the night. I felt safe because he was.

Konrad was a strong, healthy baby, and, I was told, developmentally advanced. I attended the Nanaimo Building Better Babies program and took him to my 12-step programs. He grew up in those rooms.

When he was six months old, I started feeding him solid foods. Everything was so much easier because we were living in Arno's family's big farmhouse. I'd named my baby after Arno's father, Konrad Stockhausen. He was the first man I had ever encountered who personified the real definition of a man: kind, polite, responsible, reliable, intelligent, and empathetic. He could have a disagreement with a person without being cruel and lashing out. I admired the relationship he had with his wife—he treated her with kindness and respect. I used to watch him—even study him—because I had never seen anything like it.

The name: Konrad. I thought, "It's a good German name, and my son is at least part German."

Arno was an introvert. He didn't talk much; he rarely asked for what he wanted. I guessed that he might be autistic. Something about him felt off.

I remember telling Arno one day that I wanted a home of our own—just the three of us. My motivation went farther than wanting to own property—it was also about his parents. Eventually, they would discover that Konrad was not Arno's, even if it took them years. I didn't want to live a lie. But when I told Arno that I'd like our own house one day, he said no.

His refusal disturbed me. One of my core values was stability—living under his parents' roof and rules left me feeling vulnerable: my home could be ripped away from me in an instant.

I started looking for ways to be more independent and self-reliant. The first big step I took was training to become a hypnotherapist.

I'd come to hypnotherapy on another winding road. I'd done talk therapy, and every time I came away from a session, I still had anxiety—the nervous twitch refused to disappear. I still had a deep sense of revulsion and fear. I would still leave sessions feeling like shit. Talking polished my problems—made them gleam—but they never disappeared. They just looked better.

I recalled that when I was 16, I had bought a Louise Hay book, titled *You Can Heal Your Life*, which laid out your problems and then exposed the possible Subconscious messages that might cause them. It explained the subconscious therapy needed to erase the messages and the problems. But how do you enter your own mind and repair it?

Years later and months after Konrad was born, I was teaching fitness classes again. In one centre where I worked, I met a woman who had recently been certified as a hypnotherapist. The style she had learned was authoritarian, controlling, and aggressive. But when she offered me a free session, I said yes. Why not?

She put me into a trance in a physically aggressive way where I smacked myself in the head, and on the command to sleep, I fell into that deep state. I felt like I was back in the womb. It was wonderful. And while I loved the feeling, I didn't like her approach. It was self-serving and manipulative. While I was in the state of sleep, she commanded me to take three sessions every week for three weeks. She thought I was under so deep that I wouldn't remember the command. But I did and lost all respect for her. Still, the memory of that womb-like place was so lovely and enriching that I thought, "I'll never do drugs again. If I can feel this good without putting an artificial substance in my body—then wow! I want this!"

But I wanted more than sessions. I wanted to give this gift to others. I attended the same school as my colleague and discovered why she had been so aggressive in her technique. She was following the example of her teacher. Allen Dell was a sexual predator who took advantage of his students. He also lied, telling people they would make $60,000 per annum easily after graduating. On top of all that, he was also a narcissist. At some point, he lost his licence and had to leave the province. I quit his class after a few months of training, understanding that he was never going to give me the knowledge I needed to become a good therapist.

My hunt began. I searched out hypnotherapists and attended sessions. How good was my experience? Some were better than others. I met Lance Tomlin, a highly skilled therapist. In the session, he focused on justice. He had me envision being in a courtroom where I told the room what my dad had done to me—and my dad had to pay penance. In this place, a higher justice existed. I didn't have to do anything—this was universal law.

After that session, I wept so hard that sobs wracked my whole body. I felt validated in a way I never had. All my life, people had told me I was crazy and that everything had been my fault. After that session, I lay on the floor in the house for three days, wrapped in my duvet, with a tsunami of emotions washing over me.

Lance sent me to the Orca Institute, which teaches an Ericksonian-style hypnotherapy. Milton Erickson, a psychiatrist, developed the method, designing it for doctors. In fact, when it was first introduced, only qualified physicians could enrol. This was a sophisticated approach. Milton Erickson, who is world-renowned, took hypnosis off the stage and developed it into a therapeutic tool. People who didn't do well in talk therapy—who couldn't solve their issues by prettying them up—thrived under this therapy. A good hypnotherapist won't help you manage the prickly bush of your problems; they'll help you pull it out by the roots.

Sheldon, a genuine, self-effacing, Charlie Brown sort of man, ran the Orca Institute and was a member of the Canadian Hypnosis Association—and he opened a new door for me. One course prerequisite was 850 practice hours just to get your residency and then many more hours in order to get your clinical certificate. I jumped in. When I had to have a mentor for my practicum, I found Fatah Taylor, the only practitioner in our area. He not only mentored me; he became something of a surrogate father for 15 years.

He said to me, "If you want to help people, you must do your own inner work every day. It's like winding up an old-fashioned clock. Every morning you do that work, and for the next 24 hours, that clock works properly."

I listened and followed his advice. He taught me how to do effective programming on my own because I couldn't afford to see a therapist regularly. He was adamant that I had to make an impression on my subconscious, which is most suggestible in the morning and at night before going to bed. These are times to plant the seeds, he said. So, with Fatah, I was getting support that helped me learn how to reconnect with myself and become an advocate for me. I didn't have to live a life where I did whatever everyone else wanted.

I did everything I could to become a well-functioning person who helped people, and I even got paid for it. And as I got healthier and stronger, my relationship with Arno fell apart.

But Konrad was thriving. He was so cute and fun. I recall a time when I was sitting in the living room and realized, *Hey—it's too quiet! Something's wrong.*

I got up and walked into the kitchen where I found him—he had pulled a giant bag of flour out of the cupboard and dumped most of it on the floor. So there he was, sitting on the floor in his diaper, covered in white powder, his legs kicking in joy. He was so precious that all I could do was giggle.

I had lovely moments with my boy, and I did my best to support him and to make him feel safe—that was all that mattered to me.

Of course, life wasn't entirely blissful. I couldn't feed Konrad in his high chair because it brought on acute anxiety. When I tried, I couldn't hold the spoon because I was shaking so hard and gasping for breath. I called my mother, "I can't feed Konrad in his high chair because I keep shaking. I should be enjoying this."

She wept.

"Why are you crying?" I asked her.

"Your father strangled you twice in the high chair, almost to the point of dying, because you wouldn't stop crying. I had to break a lamp over his skull, and I had to throw water on you because your eyes had rolled to the back of your head and you had turned blue."

We didn't have family dinners—the kind where you set the table and everyone sits down together at the end of the day. But I loved my baby boy and did my best to look after him. I wanted more for his future. I didn't worry about mine—it was his that I would fight for.

I let some time pass and then once again, I told Arno that I wanted a house because I wanted something to leave for my baby in case I died. In reply, Arno screamed and threw a chair at me.

"Well," I said. "At least I know how you really feel."

So I moved into a tiny A-frame cottage in Cedar' where I lived for about 18 months. I cried a lot in that small place because so many of the emotions I had buried for years began to come to the surface. I remember lying on the bed, just weeping.

I continued to work long hours on my fitness classes and hypnotherapy practice, building my confidence, but I also becoming a workaholic. "No" was not a word in my vocabulary because turning down a class meant the threat of replacement. Those classes were my primary source of income.

The anxiety and the long hours took their toll. I contracted pneumonia. I was so weak I couldn't get up, but I still had a toddler running around, spilling his sippy cup, demanding attention, needing to be fed—and all I wanted was just enough energy to pour a glass of water and buy a few pieces of fruit.

One day I was lying in bed, thinking, *I'm sick. I'm not getting paid. They'll replace me.*

Panicking at the thought, I called Arno and asked him to bring me some fruit and water—and he did.

After he left, I thought, *This is not the way I want to live my life. I'm here, feeling like this because I'm afraid of saying "no"—and yet I have to say no because I don't know how to look after myself.* When I saw my dilemma, I made a commitment that I would take at least two weeks of real vacation time every year. Somehow, I would earn enough money to do that, and I would hide it so that if I was going to have two weeks lying on my back, it was because I was having a wonderful time, not because I was sick with pneumonia.

I recovered and went back to work, and in my free time, I did deep, therapeutic soul work in that little cabin. After almost two years there, I moved into town. By then, I had started dating a man I had met in a 12-step program. I should have listened to the old joke that goes like this: *How do you get lucky at a 12-step function? You go home alone.*

But I didn't pay attention to that advice. Ray had a crush on me, and I liked him. Konrad did not—and maybe I should have paid more attention to that too. But because I had no self-confidence, Ray helped me find a place in town. Going out there and asking someone to let me look at an apartment terrified me. I couldn't do it. I suspect my fear stemmed from my experiences with my mother renting and the sexual abuse she had endured from the landlords. I was afraid of someone going after my child or coming for both of us.

So I asked Ray if he would look for me. He did and found a place right near the hospital.

By this time, I noticed that the work I had been doing with Fatah had allowed me to tap deeply into my intuition—and I was becoming almost what I would call psychic. I could communicate with disembodied souls.

Ray's daughter, Haley, had died when she was four years old. He told me it was because of the vaccinations she'd had. She died in the hospital, screaming for him while he was dealing drugs on the street. He hated himself for that, and I didn't think he had ever forgiven himself.

One day we were lying on my bed when I felt Haley's energy near me like a ball of light. Silently I asked, "Who are you?"

"Haley."

"What was your favourite fruit when you had your body?" I asked.

"Oranges."

"What was your dad's favourite activity?"

"Golf."

I talked to her more, and then I asked Ray, "What was your daughter's favourite fruit?"

"Oranges."

"What was your favourite activity when she was here?"

"Golf."

"She's here," I said. "She has something to say to you..." and he turned white and tore out of the apartment.

So sometimes I use this ability, and sometimes I don't, but at the time I didn't realize how powerful this gift was.

Fatah taught me a sacred garden exercise where you create a healing space for yourself—a space that is beautiful and just yours. In the garden, you have a building filled with all the tools you need, and in the garden are all your guides, there to help you heal.

If you're in conflict with someone, you bring them into your space, discuss it with them, and clear the issue. In that place, you also create an image of your ideal self and you remove any obstacles that prevent you from manifesting your ideal self. The second stage of this meditation is creating a path to someone else's garden—so I created a path to Ray's garden. I went there and saw that he had hung himself from a tree and that he was near death. I pulled him down and tried to revive him, but then I understood that this was my subconscious showing me the state of his being.

I hadn't realized that he was still using drugs.

Shortly after I had that vision, he crept into my apartment and stole all the money I had put away for a Disneyland trip for Konrad and me. He took my jewellery and my van as well.

Four days later, he came back, the whites of his eyes red with blood. He'd overdosed and had a grand mal seizure, and he had spent all my money. Maybe I should have been more upset, but I was just relieved that he'd brought my van back. After that, he disappeared and I never saw him again.

The incident shocked me. I had no idea he could do something like that. I think what disturbed me most was the belief that I should have known.

So once again I picked up the pieces of my life—working and teaching. Konrad was almost old enough for school now. Occasionally we would visit my mother, and once in a rare while, Konrad would stay with her for the weekend. I kept saving money, and I still had $28,000 from an ICBC claim that I'd carefully squirrelled away, so I began thinking about buying an apartment or a townhouse. But I didn't think I would qualify for a mortgage. My job wasn't stable because it depended on my physical ability.

Then one day, Inge, who I'd rented the cabin from in Cedar, introduced me to Ev Schmidt, a local realtor who took me on a tour through various residential complexes. One day we looked at a townhouse in Cedar Grove Villas, right behind Northridge Shopping Centre in Nanaimo. It was brand new and beautiful, and I loved it. And because there was a private space for an office where I could practice hypnotherapy, it was ideal.

By showing me this amazing place, I thought Ev was trying to make me feel inadequate and ashamed. After all, I could never qualify for it or be able to afford it. I didn't deserve to be in a place that nice. But she brought me to CIBC and, just like that, I was approved for a mortgage. I was in shock because this place was brand new. Everything was white. Everything was clean.

Konrad and I moved in and first I set up my office. But I still couldn't bring myself to unpack, unable to fathom that this was real. I slept on the carpet in the living room in the middle of the floor for six weeks, waiting for someone to come to the door to tell me I was not allowed to be there—to tell me I had to leave because I was the wrong kind of person for a place this nice.

Finally, I bought furniture. And while I created this home, I waited for a phone call that never came. My parents didn't telephone to say congratulations. I had bought a home! By myself! They didn't call. They didn't even acknowledge that I had done this. Once again, I felt betrayed.

But I stayed in touch, and Konrad continued his visits to my mom. But one day, when I picked him up, he clung to me like a spider—grabbing me, pulling at me, holding on as tight as he could. I asked my mother what had happened, but she just shook her head.

Something had occurred. Konrad had experienced trauma. I didn't know what it was, and I wasn't sure if he knew, but if someone had done something, it would have been my mother. She didn't understand that people had needs. She would blame them. When I left my dog with her once, she blamed the dog when he was sick. She couldn't look at the dog, realize he was sick, and then understand that he needed help. So if she couldn't do that with an animal, she wouldn't do it for a human either.

In those days, I was still in touch with Terrill, one of Ray's old friends. Terrill was a finishing carpenter who had crafted a stately grandfather clock that he couldn't bring with him when he moved house. I was thrilled to buy it because it represented family, culture, and connection.

We started dating. He treated me well, doing everything he could to show me what a great guy he was. He had a sense of humour and he had working skills, so I was convinced that he was a good man. But I was clear with him right from the start: "I'm not going to be in a relationship with you unless you want a real relationship. I'm not going to be a convenient girlfriend."

He took me to Lethbridge, Alberta, to meet his mother, who I thought was the most amazing woman. She rode a motorcycle; she had roller blades; she listened to Janis Joplin; she was an artist; she loved learning. She'd had a hard life, but she'd ended up creating a good one. She impressed me. And I was even more impressed that Terrill obviously loved his mother, and that's what I wanted—to be with someone who loved his mom. I'd learned that if you're with someone who hates their mother, they will eventually take it out on you.

We got engaged. I introduced him to Fatah, who gave him his blessing. "That's a great guy you've got," he said. "You should go forward with him. Good solid guy. Good boyfriend for you."

And that was the final piece I needed. I pulled my walls down. I was safe. We got married on Valentine's Day, went to the Bungee Zone, and jumped off together in all our wedding finery. It was my leap of faith.

The time was now right for me to take another leap. I had a body image and eating disorder; I had sexual abuse issues. I remembered, when I was young, looking at women competing in bodybuilding events on television. I thought, *Once you can do that, you no longer have a body image or food problem. You're no longer a binge eater.*

I'd made the original decision when I was 17. If I could do that and do that well, I would have proof that

I was no longer out of control with food. I had so much shame around my body and I didn't understand why. But if someone said to me, "You look good," I would put on 30 pounds. I would protect myself by getting as fat as I could tolerate, and then I would exercise to try to get the weight off. I did that over and over and over. Bodybuilding represented mastery.

My first show: I worked with Joanna Dunn, who owned Fitness Edge. I was teaching for her, and one day, she said, "There's a show coming up in Chilliwack—would you like to compete?"

I said, "I would love to as long as I don't look stupid on stage. I want to look like I belong."

I knew what it symbolized for me, and because I was married, I felt that I had a stable enough life that I could devote the time to it.

Joanna set out the regimen for me, and I prepared hard for ten weeks. When the day came, I drove to Chilliwack, crying in the car, realizing that one of my dreams was coming true because I had followed through. Not knowing what would happen on the stage unnerved me, but I was all in. This met my need for intensity and adventure, and I was being a bit of a rebel. But this competition also meant that I could go out there in a bikini and no one could touch me. No one could rape me; no one could violate me.

I was saying, "Fuck you! This is mine!"

There were nine women in the show, and I placed third. It was such a rush—and when I saw my pictures, I looked so good that I cried. I wasn't particularly muscular, but in the pictures the photographer took—the poses he showed—I looked hungry and angry, and I loved it.

When I reviewed the photographs, I got the bug. I competed a few more times and hired a trainer, Sandra Froer, to get me ready for a show in Toronto. She trained me for nine months. She had also been a professional bodybuilder, and she would train me so hard that I would say to her, "If I can't walk after this, I'm going to have to kill you."

She laughed and said, "If you want things to be different, get comfortable being uncomfortable."

In a way, she mothered me. When I was ready for Toronto, I thought, *I have never looked this good in my life.*

In Toronto, I placed first in the novice category and third in my weight category.

Meanwhile, Joanna wanted to train me to compete against her, and I said, "Absolutely not. That's a complete conflict of interest. I'm doing this just for me."

That's when she started trying to undermine me.

Not that it mattered much to me. When I saw the photos from the Toronto show, I was amazed: I looked lean and hard and amazing.

I competed a few more times on and off until I was involved in a car accident. After that, I didn't think I could ever do it again. I didn't believe I could load my upper body any longer because I had significantly damaged my neck.

But while I was engrossed in bodybuilding, I discovered that I had built my marriage on unstable ground. There were things I didn't know about Terrill until after we had married. He had a drug problem that he kept well hidden.

We bought a lot near the university almost right away and started building a big house. The bank gave us a loan on the promise that we would build the house and sell it for a good profit. Terrill was a professional carpenter, so it was a perfect scheme.

What I didn't know was that he was stealing money that was earmarked for construction expenses. We were getting close to lockup—still waiting for the windows and for the driveway to be paved—and we came to a dead stop. The money was gone: $60 000 was missing. So we had to sell my townhouse and move in because we couldn't put this big, unfinished house on the market.

While Terrill finished the house, I worked doubly hard to make as much money as possible to pay down the extra that the house was costing. Terrill never had money and there was always a reason—always a story. Someone wasn't paying him, or the money was gone for something else.

Over time, I lent him more than $20,000 that he couldn't pay back. Then he wanted me to put him on my credit card.

"You're fucking nuts," I said. "I'm not doing that. I'm not giving you a card that I have to pay for. That doesn't work."

Our only joint bank account was for mortgage payments through the Chemainus Credit Union. I was doubling and even tripling up on mortgage payments because I wanted to be debt-free as quickly as possible, but what I didn't know was that Terrill was withdrawing that money with my bank card in $500 chunks—and then he gave it back to me to make me think he was helping with payments.

I knew nothing about it until my bookkeeper alerted me. "Where is all this money that's coming out of the account?" she asked.

I had no idea. I never used my card to take money out of an ATM.

So one day, I opened a piece of mail—something I never did. All my bills and receipts went directly to my bookkeeper. I had never wanted to deal with it. I was afraid that if I opened that mail, it would inevitably be bad news. So I avoided it. This time, I opened it—inside was a statement showing that a bank account that should have a lot of money had a zero balance. I called the bank and explained, "There's a problem. This statement is incorrect."

"No, it's correct," they said.

"But I don't take money out," I said.

Then I called the Credit Union and asked for the status of my accounts. She told me and mentioned that $500 had been withdrawn earlier that day.

"But I haven't left home," I said, and I started crying because it filtered into my consciousness that Terrill had been taking my bank cards and returning them at the end of the day. He'd figured out my password—the same for every account.

Luckily, the bank manager was one of my clients; he checked the security camera; the footage showed Terrill at the ATM.

When I confronted Terrill, he said I was crazy—he wouldn't do that—had never done that. Of course, it was a lie.

Four days later, a bailiff came to the house and took my car. Terrill had done a business deal, had put my name on it, hadn't paid what he owed, and had allowed it to go to collections. I was the only one who had a good car. I was on my way to an appointment, and there was the tow truck.

"Who are you?" I asked. "What are you doing?"

The man said, "I could walk into your house and take all of your appliances."

"I don't understand," I said.

He showed me the documents from the court hearing and towed my car. I felt like my life was falling apart. Again. At the same time, I learned that Terrill had stolen $79 000—all the money I had been working for and saving to avoid debt.

Terrill came home that night with bags of groceries and a big smile on his face.

"Where's the car?" he asked.

"The bailiff took it," I said. "You ought to know something about that. You put my name on one of your business deals and you didn't pay the bill and now they're coming after me."

The next day I paid $700 to rescue my car from the impound lot and promised to pay off that debt. Then I went to a lawyer and handed over all the documents from the bank. "I want a divorce," I said.

My worry was that Terrill would fight me and drag it out, and I wouldn't be able to afford the battle, and I would have nowhere to live and no space to operate my business. I was afraid of being on the street.

So I squared my shoulders and said, "It goes like this: I'm going to give you $5 000 cash and you will sign over the house to me. Whatever equity you had, you've spent it. It's gone. If you don't, I will charge you civilly and you already have a criminal record—it won't look good in front of a judge. And I'll give you a tutu and tattoo tits on your back because I'm going to give all the other prisoners chocolate bars to fuck you up the ass every day. They will rape you. I will make sure that every day in jail will be the worst day of your life. You have two choices: sign off and I will give you $5 000, or I'm going to charge you and you will go to jail."

He took the money and left. But first I told him to take all the furniture—everything that had his smell on it. I told him to just get away from me.

I had been financing that marriage by myself for seven years. He had been leeching off me and I hadn't known it. There was a lot I hadn't known. Near the end, I was getting phone calls from people telling me that he was picking up prostitutes downtown. When I confronted him with that, he said, "I'm just trying to help them out."

"Yeah—I'll bet you are."

It all came out—his addiction to pornography on the internet, women, cocaine—all of it. He was a pathological liar. And when I told his mother what he had done, she said, "Of course he did. He's a perfectly fine criminal."

"If you knew that, why didn't you tell me before I married him?" I asked.

She had no answer.

Terrill disappeared and I fell apart. I was scared. Terrill had a friend who had been paid to murder someone's wife; he'd done time in jail and was out now. I was so paranoid that I would crawl on my hands and knees across the living room floor so that no one could see me through the window. Terrill was still the beneficiary in my will. How could I know where he would draw the line? Look at what he had already done!

We got a divorce. And, no surprise, he didn't pay child support like he was supposed to. He asked if I could let him off because now he had bills to pay. I wanted to have nothing to do with him. I asked for $5 000 and I would sign off.

Of course, the money came from a woman. I saw on Facebook that they were engaged, and I thought, *Yeah—I know how this will end.*

Maybe I should have known that he was a professional con man, but I had no insight into men—I had no instinct around them or around boundaries. I was young and naïve, and I wanted to believe in something good happening to me.

CHAPTER 4

After Terrill left, I was single for about a year and a half. I was lonely, with low self-esteem, and I thought I'd be happy if I met someone who was a good person. One day, a friend, Bill Bird said, "I have the perfect person for you."

He introduced me to Ellis, who was about nine years older than me. He had made some bad choices in his life but anchored me in the belief that if you help people they will evolve because that was what had happened to me with Fatah. He had given me support and an environment in which I could grow. And I did—I gave back wherever I could. I once said to Fatah, "How can I ever thank you for what you've done for me?"

His answer was, "Just love yourself." He was never inappropriate with me. He was only ever kind and generous. I wanted to create that same opportunity for people, but I soon realized that you shouldn't do that with a potential love interest.

Ellis and I met at a coffee shop. I had the foresight to bring along a questionnaire to determine his enneagram style, or personality traits. I thought that would tell me a lot more about him than a simple conversation. He filled in the page, showing himself to be an enneagram eight, which is a leader and a peacemaker—kind of like a fuzzy bear with teeth.

And so we talked, and because I was lonely and wanted connection, I allowed myself to get close to him quickly—much too soon. We became intimate before I knew that he didn't have his own home, that he was living in his car or couch-surfing at friends' houses.

The 9/11 crisis had ruined him. He'd been involved in a multi-level marketing company selling products from Japan, and he'd spent years building it up and investing all his money. He thought he'd built an empire, and then the bottom fell out.

I didn't know any of this for some time. I was such a good caretaker, I said, "You can stay at my house until you get on your feet—until you get a job."

That was the end of the honeymoon phase. Because of his situation, he complained about everything. He told me how grateful I should be that I was doing so well as a self-employed person.

Feeling trapped, hopeless, numb, and disassociated, I went to a therapist. I wanted Ellis out. I asked him to move a number of times, but he would humiliate me or shame me, making me feel that I was a bad person for wanting him to go. I wanted a relationship where we could get to know each other; instead, we were glued together all day. His way of trying to make it better was cooking meals and doing chores around the house, but it felt like he was being a controller. And everything he did, he did grudgingly.

Despite this, he was a good man in many ways, but I also felt that he had conned me. The equity in my house was another concern because once we had been living together for two years, the law entitled him to a percentage of it.

Then Ellis introduced me to a woman involved in a company called The Institute for Financial Freedom. Like Ellis, Debbie had come from the multi-level marketing world and had done well until 9/11 and the collapse of the markets.

She told a miraculous story about an educational program that led to access to investments that normally only wealthy people could take part in. I was curious. Why wouldn't I want that benefit?

So I paid $1 800 to go to Calgary and participate in a head-hunting process that involved me in investment funds that the company placed offshore. I was fascinated. According to them, I could retire in five years on a passive income of about $5 000 per month. And then Ellis might stop complaining and we could just have a good time. Everything would become easy.

They based the fund on the model rich people use to invest their money offshore, avoiding taxes and reaping all the benefits. I was introduced to the founder of the company, Milo Brost, and his partner, Gary Sorenson, who owned a group of high-yielding gold mines in Ecuador and Honduras. I also met investors who had been with the partners for years—people who travelled like jet setters, going to Europe, buying expensive cars, and living the life.

Well, I thought, *Why not me?*

I invested all the money I had saved for my retirement and took the equity I could pull out of the house and invested that too for a total of about $220 000. I was so convinced about this scheme that I recommended it to others, including my mother and stepfather.

It didn't end well. Instead of bringing in legitimate wealth, it turned out to be one of the biggest scams in Canadian history. I lost all my money. My friends lost all theirs—and that was a source of horrific shame, self-loathing, and guilt. I wanted to punish myself for the cash they had lost. It was all my fault, wasn't it?

Milo and Gary went to jail. The investigation showed that they had run a Ponzi scheme that had genuine professional financial advisers involved. Sure, I had done due diligence, but not nearly enough. I was greedy. If I had invested the minimum of $50 000, I would not have lost everything. I would not have ended up with a giant hole in my finances. The Canadian Securities Commission dug deep. All the "secure" money had vanished. All the mining companies with proven reserves were a lie. People who had sold everything—their houses, farms, and businesses—all for the opportunity presented to them—committed suicide.

With all this going on, I had bowed out of my personal training business downtown. Overworked, unhappy, and not making enough money, I sold the business to the head trainer, who was sure that he'd make an easy go of it.

"Talk to me over lunch in nine months," I said. He didn't know how hard the work was and how many bills there were each month. It was so difficult to stay ahead.

The stress was too much. I told the trainer, "If I don't get out of this, I'm going to get cancer—I'm so unhappy."

My failed investment made me angry, but more than that, afraid. I remember weeding the front yard, putting all my energy into yanking out dandelions and hawkweed, knowing how much trouble I was in: all the equity in my house—gone. At the very least, Ellis couldn't get it and no matter how shitty that sounds, it was one bright point.

And somehow, I was still in denial, holding on to a faint thread of hope. Maybe it would all come out right after all. So I threw myself into my work. I had to for my sanity's sake.

One day, I was driving to a client's house in Nanaimo's north end, near the big Rutherford Road hill. As I came around the tight corner on the hill, with the rain coming down, another car came towards me; the driver lost control on the slick road, crossed into my lane, and flew towards me. I aimed towards the ditch, but didn't have time to react quickly enough. He crashed into me, destroying both vehicles. I could see blood on his face and on the passenger's face. I looked down at my legs.

"Yes, they're still connected to me. Okay—that's good."

And then I shook—almost convulsing. First responders arrived. "Are you okay?"

"Yes—I'm okay."

I knew that I should go to the hospital, but fear of unemployment trumped common sense. With a dance class to teach that night, I had to get there. I didn't know that I had a concussion or that I'd sustained a spinal cord injury. *I'll heal,* I thought, *and everything would be all right.*

Through the following days, I felt worse. I had a hard time talking and putting even simple words together. My ears rang and my head felt too heavy for me to carry. I had to lie down with my head hanging over the edge of the bed.

My doctor said I'd be fine. I'd sustained soft tissue injuries and they would heal.

Ellis was angry with me because I was no longer engaged with him—or with life. I was so shut down that my son asked me, "Mommy, are you dying?"

"I don't know," I said. "But I do feel like I'm dying."

That was my life for the next two years. My bodybuilding days were done, but I still worked. I still had my clients, but between appointments, I would go upstairs and lie down, recharging as best I could. And then I started to hear voices. There was a male voice, loud and clear: "Why don't you just kill yourself? Everything will be better if you kill yourself."

I started plotting the logistics of suicide, playing out the scenes in my mind. I told myself it was just depression. I'd pull out of it. I just had to keep going. After two weeks of voices, I went to my doctor.

"Something is wrong," I told him. "I hear voices. They're not going away and they're very strong and loud. It's a male voice and I'm scared."

He sent me to a specialist for neurological evaluations; the specialist determined that I was suffering from extreme depression. My eyes burned, my hands and feet burned; I couldn't talk or think. I'd lost a lot of weight and I doubted that I could look after myself anymore.

I'd already done physiotherapy, so the specialist sent me to a psychologist. She was lovely, but her approach was to help me accept my condition as a new normal.

Really? I couldn't walk properly. I was limping and I had chronic pain in every part of my body. I had done everything I could to get better, and I was still broken. I was in so much pain that I couldn't function.

I felt isolated and afraid. I didn't want anyone to see me or talk to me. The only exception was when I was working. But even there I had problems. I could no longer trust my ability to assess the exercises to prescribe. I had a new client, the dean of the University of Lethbridge, and I looked at her and didn't know which therapeutic exercise to assign, and I knew that I didn't know. I cross-referenced my ideas three or four times before I would commit anything to paper.

I needed help, and if no one could help me, then I had to do it myself. I threw myself into research and eventually found Nora Gaddadis, a neuro-feedback and nutritional therapist who had written a book called *Primal Body, Primal Mind* about using the ketogenic diet to increase blood flow to the prefrontal cortex. She said that sugar decreased the blood flow by 30 percent. I listened to her podcast and thought that if this was true, her method would give me back some of what had disappeared.

I had nothing to lose. I couldn't even write simple words, so I tried her diet plan at a two-week intensive retreat in Mexico. I came back with my brain functioning once again. I was also calmer and my anxiety had decreased significantly.

I wanted more. She referred me to a practitioner who did biofeedback therapy in Coquitlam. I got on the ferry, and within one session, I could write proper sentences again. Parts of my brain that had shut off because of the trauma of the accident turned back on again. I invested heavily in the therapy, and it was worth every penny. But I also kept every receipt with the idea that ICBC would reimburse me one day.

But Ellis was still in my life, and I wanted him out more than ever. I did not want to move forward with this relationship. It had already started to harm me. After the car accident, he said, "You're not an addict. You're not like all those other people. You can have a glass of wine with me."

I was in pain, and I was vulnerable. So I had a glass of wine with him—after 18 years of being clean and sober. I'd lost my spiritual foundation. I'd lost my connection with God. I felt alone, and I turned to alcohol to manage the sadness and disappointment in my life. Somewhere inside, I knew it wouldn't help—in fact, it only made everything worse. I suffered from the after-effects of the accident, and now I had alcohol and a man I didn't want in my life.

I remember sitting across from him one day saying, "One of us has to leave, or one of us is going to get killed. I'm done."

"Well," he said. "You're going to have to give me a percentage of your ICBC claim and I want a percentage of the equity in your house."

I looked him straight in the eye. "Five thousand dollars is all it would take for you to disappear and for a bullet to be found in the back of your head."

He emailed his sister. "If I'm found dead or if I'm missing, Germana has threatened my life."

I had never loved him. I don't think I knew how. We never had an honest, intimate relationship. When I met him, he told me he was a tantric master and healer. He was a sex god with years of training. It was all bullshit. But I was naïve—taken in by his handsome face and believing that he'd had some hard times, and we all had those, right? Everyone deserves a second chance. But I was doing all the hard lifting. If I'd known better, I would have waited for him to sort himself out and then gone on a few dates with him.

But I had no boundaries. He moved into my home and then, when I wanted him out, he shamed me into letting him stay. I kept letting it go, hoping it would all turn out okay. But it wasn't okay—not ever.

So now I was drinking, and my doctor had put me on morphine to handle my pain. And I was so scared. I knew what it was to be an addict—I knew about that life. And I had no support system—no one to go to. I'd lost my recovery community, and there was no one in my family I could turn to. All I had was my physiotherapist and occupational therapist.

I sincerely wanted to die. But I couldn't do that to my son—and that led to the conversation at the kitchen table: "One of us is leaving or dying."

He left. I had to pay him $50 000 to leave because that was his threat: "I won't leave unless you give me this amount of money."

He also wanted a percentage of my ICBC claim.

"What makes you think you're entitled to anything?" I asked. "I'm the one with the broken body."

"I've had to live with you," he said.

"What about me? I've had to live with me," I said. "Because I'm not Miss Happy and Bubbly anymore, you want to be paid? Go ahead—go to ICBC and see if you're entitled to anything. The lawyer gets 30 percent. You're not getting anything that's leftover—that's for me."

I went to the bank, refinanced the house, and gave him $50 000. I told him he was a scumbag and a bottom feeder and some other things I'm not proud of.

One of the things that stuck in my mind, the thing that was the last piece of impetus I needed to ask him to leave, was the question of a dog. I wanted a little dog.

"You can't have a dog until my dog dies," he said. "And it will take at least three years after that—I will need time to grieve."

I wanted a dog—a companion that would make me want to be alive again and his response was "no." I flipped. That pushed my button. That was the final thing that made me determined to get him out.

With Ellis gone, I went to a breeder in Chemainus and got a Pomeranian puppy that I named Jazz. He was beautiful, cute, and a complete sweetie. I looked after him—made sure he had a strong sense of his value and his worth. He was safe and loved and nourished. I needed to give and receive that unconditional love.

But I also fell back into my old patterns. As soon as I broke off with Ellis, I fell into another intimate relationship with Michael, an old school friend from my days in Maple Ridge. He was a way of assuring myself that the connection with Ellis was truly severed.

Michael presented himself as a macho guy who had his shit together. But it was just an act.

When he was younger, he used to fly with his dad in a small plane. One day, the plane crashed, and he watched his father die while he waited for the first responders to arrive. When he reached the age of 18, he inherited a sizable trust fund from his father.

He used the money to buy drugs, fast cars, motorcycles, and women. That was his world. He was a giant tapeworm, consuming everything he could. He overdosed on LSD once and probably sustained some brain damage. He was certainly institutionalized at least once.

The first time I visited him, he tried to hide the fact that he had an artificial leg. Maybe that should have told me something. But I poked it. "What happened to your leg?" I asked.

He told me that he had been high on drugs and drunk and riding one of his Harleys, ran a red light, and was rammed by a car. His leg was crushed and had to be amputated. He told me that he raged, threatening to kill the doctor and nurses for not saving his leg. I listened, sitting in his nice house by the big bay window, and then I noticed a loaded gun on the windowsill.

"Michael," I said. "That's a loaded gun."

"Yeah—I just shoot the birds once in a while," he said.

I knew it was a lie, knew he was a murderer. "I think you've used it on people from time to time," I said.

"Yeah—I fired at a guy down by the mailboxes," he admitted. "Put a bullet through his head. The cops came by, but they couldn't prove anything."

I was sure there was more than one. But it didn't scare me away. I wanted comfort. And he was injured—just like me. We had that in common.

One day, he took me to an outdoor party at the Black Swan Pub. That evening, one of the girls took me aside and said, "What are you doing with him? He's crazy. You need to get away from him as quickly as possible."

Thanks to her, the red flag finally went up, and I connected some dots: crazy; gun; shot someone by the mailboxes; missing a leg and he tries to hide it; and, taking a lot of steroids. *Okay, this guy is bad for me.* But at least he was in Maple Ridge and didn't know where I lived on the island. I didn't want him to show up at my house. That was one boundary I didn't want him to cross.

There was also the part of me that wanted to help. His father had died. His sister had committed suicide. Someone else in the family had died, so he had lots of grief and destructive coping strategies. He had a young son who was also struggling with drugs. One day, the boy's mother called, and I could hear her across the room screaming at her son, who was high on drugs. "I hope you fucking die! I hate your fucking guts!"

She was saying that to her baby.

I wanted to help Michael. I wanted to pay for him to have biofeedback sessions. But long before anything could happen, someone Michael knew called him and said that his son had choked on his own vomit and asphyxiated. The ambulance had taken him to the hospital.

"He's dead," I said to Michael. "We have to go to the hospital."

Michael was drunk and high and out of his mind. I drove him to the hospital in New Westminster. Michael's son was brain dead, hooked up to machines to keep him alive long enough for everyone to say goodbye.

The mother came into the room, screaming, shrieking—almost insane with rage and hostility. And I thought about the last thing her son had heard from her—that she hated his guts and wished he would die. And now he was dead.

Finally, it was time to take Michael back home. If he'd stayed at the hospital, I don't knows what damage he would have done to the doctors and nurses because they couldn't keep his son alive. I made him eat and gave him a sleeping pill. As soon as his eyes closed, I left and got on the ferry.

When I got home, I hugged my son and asked him why he didn't take drugs.

"Mom," he said. "You told me your story."

The next time I talked to Michael, he wanted me to give him a baby. No—that was definitely not for me. But that summer, I rented a nice hotel room in downtown Vancouver at the Sheraton Wall and invited Michael for what I hoped would be a romantic weekend away. He destroyed the room and attacked me. That's when I knew that he was evil and I was in trouble. Later that night, when he was asleep, I packed my things and escaped. I realized at that point that he hated women. And I understood something else: Michael was just like my dad. It was the same energy, the same personality style: Dr. Jekyll and Mr. Hyde.

He texted me when he woke up: "Where are you?"

My response was, "You hurt me. You're never going to have another opportunity to do that again."

Meanwhile, I continued to struggle with the recovery from the accident, and I finally brought myself back to a 12-step program. But my nervous system was still so sensitive and off-kilter that I couldn't sit in any of those rooms without shaking. I would actually vibrate. I hadn't slept for nine months after the accident—I just sat up at night shaking—and I was still shaking.

One day, I sat beside a big guy in one of the rooms—a guy who had been in long-term recovery. I was shaking and crying, and he kissed me on top of the head and said, "It's going to be okay."

I didn't quite believe him, but I looked at him and thought maybe I would be okay—but only if I stayed with the program.

He asked me, "Is there anything I can do to help you?"

I knew he had a Harley, so I said, "Take me for a ride on your motorcycle."

"Sure," he said. "No problem."

His name was Dave Ray and, as promised, he came over to my house and took me for a ride. As soon as I got on the motorcycle, I was so distracted by the sun and the wind and the speed that I couldn't feel any pain. There was no pain!

Dave introduced me to Sober Riders, a recovery group for motorcycle riders. I wanted to go to Narcotics Anonymous too, but I couldn't—not as long as I was on pain pills. I had stopped drinking, but I was on morphine. I couldn't function without it and I was ashamed.

The people at Sober Riders were a lot like the people I used to hang out with when I did a lot of drugs—but they weren't doing drugs or alcohol. They were giant, older kids. And I was okay with that.

I met a woman there who attended with her husband. They each had a motorcycle. "If you stay sober, you can do anything," she told me.

I looked at her long and hard. *I want a motorcycle*, I thought. *If you can do it, so can I.*

I had also been doing some online dating and met a guy named Colin who was a beautiful man. We had sex right away. And that was all he wanted. But me—I had it bad for him. I thought he was everything I'd ever wanted in a man—he even rode a motorcycle. When he rejected me,

I felt worthless, dirty, bad, and ashamed. I was not good enough. Something was wrong with me.

It was Colin who took me to the Harley-Davidson dealership to look at bikes. I found the one I wanted and took pictures of it. I promised myself that my amends to myself, at some point, would include buying myself a motorcycle.

I was deep into recovery now. Val, my original sponsor who I trusted with my life, was there for me. One day, she came over and I confessed about the medication I was taking. I was so afraid of her reaction that I could hardly breathe. I was so terrified of anyone knowing. My role was as a professional fitness person. I was supposed to help people. I wasn't supposed to be taking drugs. I had a persona—I had my shit together—but behind the scenes, I was a fucking mess.

Val looked at me and said, "Your addiction has you by the jugular and you don't even know it. You're on very strong medication and you need to go on medical detox."

I told my doctor, "I want to go on medical detox. I want to get off this medication."

He laughed at me. "You're taking as much medication as a baby Aspirin. Just take some Tylenol."

I booked off work for two weeks and flew to Cabo San Lucas to detox. On day three, I felt like I had a mild flu, and then it was over. I'd been so afraid of the pain and as I got the medication out of my system, I felt less pain. I was better able to monitor what my body could tolerate.

Based on that detox, my clean date was December 20, 2013.

I finally felt that I could go back to Narcotics Anonymous. I no longer had to hang my head in shame.

I still had a lot of emotional anxiety. I still couldn't handle stress well. I still felt shame and humiliation, but I knew that if I stayed on the program, I had a chance. On my own, I would be a mess. These 12-step programs made my life work. Otherwise, I knew I would once again make poor choices. I didn't know how to make good choices. I had my story, and my story dominated my thinking and coping, and it informed how little I believed in myself.

CHAPTER 5

While I was in Mexico, my ICBC settlement arrived. The government insurer had been chasing me with private investigators because they didn't believe I was in such trouble and so much pain.

Whenever I saw cars tailing me, I called my lawyer. "Tell that insurance adjuster to get this tail off me, or I'll take him out of his car and punch his head off. I'm trying to put my life back together."

ICBC sent me to a forensic psychiatrist because they thought I was insane, so I made them pay me $1 500 to go. The doctor reported that I was intelligent and not crazy. ICBC wanted to give me $30 000. I told them no way. I'd lost $70 000 in the first year because I wasn't able to work properly, and I'd spent almost $50 000 on my rehab.

Next, they sent me to a neurologist in Vancouver, and again I made them pay me $1 500 for my time. He determined that I had a spinal cord injury, and that surgery could fix it. He sent ICBC a memo—and instantly my claim went from $30 000 to $100 000.

My lawyer understood that ICBC was in trouble because they had overlooked my medical issues.

A judge looked over all the reports and determined that I should be awarded $350 000. I thought it was worth more. My lawyer's assistant said, "No, we're done," and ICBC cut me a cheque.

The first thing I did was order my motorcycle: a brand new 2014 Harley-Davidson Softail Slim. It was delivered in early January and sat regally in my garage. It was so beautiful: a wine red colour—all shiny and perfect in every way. Every time I sat in my car with the garage door closed, I would roll down the windows and inhale the fresh leather and chrome and new motorcycle smell. And I would sit there and stare at it and smile and smile and smile.

I loved it, but it terrified me—and I was also so proud of myself because I had kept the promise that I would buy this bike, that I would do this for me. I'd spent about $32 000 on it, and that was scary—but I was so proud.

I remember straddling the bike at the top of the driveway, the garage door open, turning the key, listening to the thunk-thunk of the motor, and I'm sure I said "Wow!" out loud. I would sit there and imagine taking it down the drive and turning right up the street until I thought, *If I pull the clutch out and I don't control it, I'm going to become part of the concrete.*

And so this beautiful bike lived in my garage for a couple of months. Finally, I asked a friend who had a motorcycle licence for a referral to an instructor. They recommended a guy named Randy, who operated a motorcycle school. I already had a licence, but I knew that I had to refresh my skills, especially with this bike.

So I paid Randy $900; it was my way of taking responsibility for my life. I didn't just want to ride that bike out into the street, hoping for the best—I wanted to do it well. And so I rode one of Randy's bikes: a little 150cc that felt like a toy compared to my 1100cc Harley. But still, it was a good start.

While taking lessons, Jenna, an old friend, called me up for help. Her partner, Lyle, a retired Hell's Angel, had been in the hospital for several months. He was a big man who raced Nitro Harleys. He was diabetic, but that didn't stop him from looking after his wood developing business and from working hard –too hard.

He'd been flying back from a business trip that he'd cut short because he knew something wasn't right with his health. In the hospital, he was diagnosed with an extremely rare disease: a virus had attacked the myelin sheath on his spinal cord, and he was sinking into paralysis. He couldn't talk, he couldn't walk, and he couldn't breathe on his own. Within three weeks, he'd lost 50 pounds. The doctors told Jenna that he would die. Three times they called her and the children to his bedside to say goodbye.

In a final heroic effort, the surgeons transplanted a foreign immune system into Lyle's body, and it worked, arresting the progress of the disease, although he still couldn't walk or breathe on his own. Regaining his vital functions was a slow and painful process.

"But who is helping you with this?" I asked Jenna, knowing what a toll it had to be taking.

She burst into tears. "Can you help him walk again?"

Even today, I weep thinking of their plight and the pain she went through, staying by his side every step of the way.

They brought him into my studio in the house in a wheelchair. Patiently, I worked with him. At the beginning, he couldn't even feel his feet. We worked together for months, two or three times a week. Slowly, he got stronger. Often, I would choke up, watching the effort he put into the work.

Lyle knew bikes and when he saw mine, he said, "You got the right bike."

What a relief after hearing so many negative comments.

"How could you get a bike so big?"

"You should get a smaller bike!"

"What were you thinking?"

"Do you have any idea what you're doing?"

"You might die."

But I didn't buy a bike fearing what I could handle. I bought a bike I loved, knowing that if I'd played it safe, I'd be mad at myself every time I watched someone ride a bike that spoke to me. And would I ever have that much money again? If I'd bought a smaller bike and traded it in in six months later, goodbye to $8 000 in depreciation.

Then there was Lyle. He looked at my baby and said, "Yup, that's the right bike for you. That's the right size for you. You just need confidence."

Lyle and Jenna lived a few minutes away on a beautiful property set up for motorcycles. I taught him to walk again. He taught me to ride.

He took my brand new bike to his property, where he had a multitude of motorcycles—bikes that would go from 0 to 200 in seconds—along with a bunch of 150cc bikes and everything in between. He regained his weight: about 270 pounds.

He straddled one of his 150cc bikes. I was on my Harley monster.

"Now, pull the clutch out," he said.

And off we went.

I spent a lot of time there over the next few weeks. Lyle put me into all kinds of situations to test how well I would do. And if I dropped the bike—which I did—he'd say, "You done good. We're done for today. Come back tomorrow."

He was my mentor and my coach. Randy may have been refreshing my road skills, but Lyle was the one who made me feel that I could do it. He respected the choice I had made. We worked at it for two weeks before he said. "Okay—you're ready to ride on the road now."

For my debut ride, Lyle invited a group of friends over on their bikes and we rode out like a pack of wolves—rumbling down the highway for four hours. What a feeling. It was beyond fun. I felt like a wild animal. I was with my pack—my people. What I loved was the silence. Sure—they're noisy—but no one talks to you. They might wave or give you a hand signal but in the middle of the pack, you're alone. I felt like a ghost. I named it the "Call of the wild." When I hear a pack of bikers go by, I feel a rush—*It's time to go now. It's time to be with my people.*

I was vindicated. Yes, I had made the right choice. The way the other guys had belittled me? Screw them! I was riding with good people—quality people. They weren't drug dealers, and they weren't screwed up. These people rode motorcycles because it was fun. And I was part of their team.

I thanked Lyle and he just waved it off like it was no big deal. I told him, "You don't understand how much your support meant. You gave me the courage to believe in myself. I know what to do on a hill, in a curve, and in any situation that comes at me. You created this experience for me."

On that first day, we rode, had a meal, and came back. After that, Lyle took me for a night ride with another group to learn to ride in the dark. After that, he said, "Now you can take your bike home."

And there it was: my bike. I rode it between client appointments—I rode it every chance I got. They say it takes about 500 kilometres to get comfortable on a new bike—to get to know it intimately. Every motorcycle is unique: brakes, clutch—everything—like a human being.

A bike—especially a big bike like mine—is a dangerous toy. I knew that many people get on these things and don't respect the potential for something to go wrong. A car or truck can hit them. They can wipe out on a slippery road surface. They can lose a body part, sustain brain damage, or die.

Some of my clients said to me, "You might get hurt. You might even die."

I said, "I'll die one day anyway, and when God wants me, I'll know all about it. And I'll go. And if I get in an accident on a motorcycle, I hope I die because I don't want to go through another lengthy rehab process. I don't think I have it in me."

To those clients who feared for me, I said, "Please understand: I don't want to sit in my house and wish I had done this. I need to do it now."

Riding gave me another freedom. When I was on the bike, I felt none of the neuropathy that still plagued me. For me, riding was one big "Wow!"

I put a lot of kilometres on that bike in a very short period of time.

One of my riding buddies, Claire, had purchased a small bike because she'd bought into everyone else's fears. Lyle had addressed that for me. He'd said, "Once it's moving, it doesn't matter how big the engine is. It's like a pedal bike, but it's got an engine in it." He removed the whole fear factor about the amount of power it had.

After one tiring day, I found Claire at the bottom of my driveway on her little bike waiting for me. Exhausted, I pulled the bike out of the garage and from there, I'm not sure what happened. I pulled the clutch and hit the throttle, and then I let go and the bike flew away, crashed on its side, and bounced down the drive, coming to rest at the bottom.

Thank God I'd let go of it because I could have been dragged right under that machine. But the poor bike: it was leaking oil, the handlebars were all twisted, the headlight was bent—and God knows what else. It took a tremendous effort to keep breathing and not lose it.

I called a friend who came over right away and pulled the bike upright. I wasn't strong enough to pick it up, not with my emotions all over the place—mostly grief for my beautiful machine.

I called Lyle and told him what had happened. "It's good that you weren't on it," he said. "Everyone's going to have one accident. At least yours happened in your driveway."

He told me to take it to RE Cycle for repairs. I could trust them. I also called the insurance company. I had a $300 deductible and there was at least $14 000 in damages. With that taken care of, my friend said, "You've got to get on it right away; otherwise, you'll never ride again."

I got back on it. For the next three days, I drove around with bent handlebars and a skewed headlight, and a bunch of other things out of whack. But I forced myself to ride it before taking it to the shop.

When it came back, a lot of it was brand new: tank, primary case, handlebars—they had replaced every single thing I had damaged. I started riding a lot, and I dropped it a few times at stoplights. But I kept riding.

Sometimes I rode with people in the recovery community. I hadn't realized that riding a massive Harley intimidated some guys. And some were jealous. They tried to spread rumours that I was a dangerous rider. But other people who rode with me heard the talk and said, "No—she's a really good rider."

But these guys with the rumours thought, *Who is this woman to come back into these rooms after relapsing, having a spinal cord injury and a thyroid injury—and besides, she's a little bit crazy—and she bought a bike.*

Most of these people were living in rental units and they had bikes they'd pieced together. Not me—I'd bought something brand new. They maltreated me because they felt threatened by me.

I just wanted to ride like everyone else and be treated like everyone else. Johnny, a guy in that community, pursued me for ages, and I finally started dating him. Shelley, a beautiful woman I rode with, said I should give him a chance. At first, I said no, then I thought, *Well, why not? It might be a lovely romantic experience.*

Johnny suffered from PTSD and took antidepressants. He had no emotional range. He didn't know how to be intimate and he couldn't orgasm. I didn't realize all this at once but it didn't take long to piece it all together.

Another woman in the recovery community—schizophrenic or bipolar or both—was rumoured to squirt when she had sex. She wanted Johnny, and Johnny broke up with me for her. I was stunned—she was a mess who didn't even pay her own way. But Johnny? He'd heard the rumours about her, and he wanted the squirting experience.

I was hurt—maybe more upset than I should have been. But if that was the kind of man Johnny was, I was better off without him.

Hanging out with Lyle and his friends made me happy. I became reacquainted with Steven Elliot, my old school friend. He worked for Lyle and he was a Hell's Angel. We hung out occasionally, but I didn't want another relationship. He often apologized to me for being a gang member. I remember sitting at my kitchen table with Steven across from me, his head hanging down, "I'm so sorry. I haven't done much with my life."

He told me that he couldn't cross the border because he was flagged. He told me that the love of his life had died, and about his failed businesses. He was still smoking, doing drugs, and drinking.

"But Stevie, you chose this," I said.

He wanted me to console him—and I could do that. I could drift in and out of disparate groups and not get entangled. Despite everything, I could still be Stevie's friend. But the word got out that I didn't want to have anything to do with these people anymore—with these drug dealers and alcoholics. I was hanging out with people who had a different lifestyle, or I was by myself.

Once in a while, I would get a call: "How come you don't hang out with us anymore? How come you're not meeting up with us at Tim Horton's?"

"I'm not interested," I said. "I don't need to be part of your group. I have little in common with you other than I ride a motorcycle and I'm in recovery."

I knew one thing: you are who your friends are. You become like the five people you spend most of your time with. I didn't want to have anything to do with what these people represented. They were disgusting. They used people, lied, and manipulated them.

I rode a lot on my own. Sometimes I rode with others—long trips like Port Hardy and back in a day. I became a gypsy girl—or, more accurately, I'd got my gypsy back, resonating with the old Fleetwood Mac lyrics:

> *So I'm back to the velvet underground*
> *Back to the floor that I love*
> *To a room with some lace and paper flowers*
> *Back to the gypsy that I was*
> *To the gypsy that I was*

My bike made me feel wild and in charge, but also not in control because the minute I let the clutch out and rode down that driveway, I would say, "God, please bring me back safe and sound. Please hover over me; fill me with grace. Protect me. Let me come home."

Every time I went out, I knew that I was risking my life, but that bike filled my driving need for intensity and adventure and even recognition. People would look at me as I rode by and I would grin at them with my pink lipstick and my pink hair sock. The bike fed my soul.

There came a time when the chrome on the bike needed to be polished and all the other parts needed a clean. But I was never a good Martha Stewart. When I dated Johnny briefly, I got him to clean my bike—one reason I kept him around—my personal bike polisher.

As we drifted into fall, near the end of the riding season, I lied to myself and told myself I would clean the bike. By then I'd put about 45 000 kilometres on it. Most people don't put that on a bike during their lifetime.

As usual, I consulted Lyle. "Lyle," I said. "When do these bikes lose their value?"

"Ah—you might get one more season out of it," he said. "You're not going to be able to trade it in for much unless you get rid of it soon."

So I took the bike to the Harley-Davidson dealership workshop on how to polish your bike. The truth was—I was not much interested in polishing.

But I rode my bike down, parked it in the lot, and started walking around—getting high on lots of recognition. I suspect I was strutting.

A sales guy came by and said hello, asked me what was going on. We chatted for a bit and then he said, "You should check out this bike over here."

It was beautiful—beyond beautiful. If you can imagine, it was like two bikes in one. It was a CVO Softail Deluxe. CVO stands for Custom Vehicle Operation and Harley-Davidson only makes a limited number of them. They are the Rolls-Royce of Harley Davidsons. It had everything, including a GPS. If you were to buy a bike and trick it out to that level, it would cost about $55 000 dollars.

I sat on it and pulled out the clutch. Surprise! It was easier to walk with than my bike. This bike was a jet compared to mine, which was more like a Sherman tank. I looked at the price tag.

"Do you like the bike?" the salesman asked.

"How much will you give me for mine?"

He inspected mine. "I'll give you $18 500."

"And what's the price on this?"

"Forty-three thousand."

"I fucking hate the paint!" I said. "It's ugly."

He frowned and looked at me with ever-so-slightly narrowed eyes. I knew that they wanted to sell it—they could only keep it at the dealership interest-free for so long.

"If we took $5 000 off, would that make the paint okay?" he asked.

"I have to phone Lyle," I said.

I called him, took a picture, and texted it to him. "How much is it?" he asked. "And how much will they give you for yours?" I told him; he was quiet for a good couple of minutes.

"Buy it," he said. "You only live once."

I ended the call, turned to the salesman, and said, "Done!"

They wasted no time: wheeled my bike into the cleaning bay, brought in the insurance man, and got the papers sorted out. I rode the new bike home.

It was so easy to handle. Everything about it was amazing. This bike was a collector's item: an 1850cc racing bike.

I might have turned heads before, but now when I rode my bike to recovery meetings, the guys' jaws dropped. I didn't really understand how special this bike was until I saw the reactions and did some research. Most people could never buy a bike like this. And if they could, they would probably talk themselves out of it.

Not me—I was all about the experience. This might have been the last bike I'd ever buy. Everything about it fit me perfectly. So I gave myself permission to ride it a lot and really enjoy it. I was the girl gypsy on the bike for the rest of that 2014 season. I never dropped that bike—not once. And I'd dropped my "Sherman tank" at least seven times. But never this one—this was my freedom jet.

CHAPTER 6

I was still attending meetings in 2014—still in my first year of recovering after my relapse. My original goal with biking had been to meet a nice man who had a motorcycle, and I would have the privilege of riding pillion. Well, the men I met in recovery weren't exactly "catches." I told one of my friends, "I'd rather take my eyeball out with a pencil and eat it."

I remember one man, Dave, saying, "You don't understand—I have a high standard in women."

I said, "Dave. Listen. We can do this the easy way or the hard way. I already said no to you and that hasn't changed. If you don't respect my boundaries, I will say something that will change your feelings about me every time you think of me. I am not interested. Period."

Then came Norm. He was young—not so much in age but in his mannerisms. I would see him at meetings, but I pointedly ignored him. I would walk past him as though he wasn't there. I judged that he was an introvert. He had serious health issues and basically he just revolted me.

Now and then I would upload training and educational videos on YouTube. Norm must have been browsing through the internet one night because he found one of my postings and discovered what I did for a living.

The next time I saw him, he asked if I would help him. I shrugged him off. "I really can't help you because you smoke," I said. Besides, I doubted he could afford my services.

Weeks later, he booked an appointment and arrived in his red Porsche, which he parked on the street in front of my house.

Okay, he had money.

He came in and bought a significant package of sessions. He would need them: he could hardly walk. Suffering from emphysema, he needed three different puffers just to keep himself on his feet. He was a wreck.

I informed him that I was off to Mexico for two weeks, but I gave him some tough initial homework.

"While I'm away, you need to stop smoking," I told him, not believing for one minute that he would.

He said, "Okay."

I flew to Cabo San Lucas with a girlfriend and another mutual friend. We rented Harleys and rode all over Cabo. We ate excellent food and hung out in the sun. It started off as a beautiful, relaxing holiday, but I discovered that my girlfriend and I were there for different reasons. I was in Cabo to relax, lie back like a big old iguana, and soak up the sun; she couldn't stop fussing and nit-picking about everything.

I said to her, "Listen, Shelley. I've saved up all year to be here for two weeks. I don't give a fuck about any of these details. I'm here to relax."

I would get up in the morning, throw on my bathing suit and a shirt, eat breakfast, and hang out. Shelley slept in until noon and then fussed with her hair, makeup, and jewellery.

One day while she was curling her hair, I said, "This is Mexico. Nobody cares. Just wave money—that makes people happy here. And if you want to get laid, you don't have to go to all this trouble."

We would walk into town and she would haggle with people selling jewellery, and I knew that these people needed to make a certain amount of money to survive. But she would spend 15 or 20 minutes grinding someone down and then walk away.

I was furious. I said to her, "These people are trying to pay their bills. Don't do that and don't drag me along with you. I'm embarrassed."

I didn't understand it. I suspected it was just a power trip for her. I was almost ready to strangle her by the time we had been there for two weeks. I escaped her by putting my headset on. One day. she threatened to catch an early flight home.

"You know," I said. "It doesn't have to be like this. You and I have different needs. I work hard all year long and you keep yourself busy with looking for part-time employment. You feel like a throwaway because you think you're too old to matter any more. We also have different economic realities. I need to rest when I'm here. Your approach to this place is stressful for me."

We hung in there for the duration. Once home, I walked in the door and all the tension I'd buried snapped; I vomited and felt a pain that brought me to my knees. The vomiting continued, increasing in intensity. It was so bad that I called an ambulance.

The hospital staff checked me for a brain tumour. The CT Scan and MRI came out clean, but they gave me steroids to stop the inflammation and sent me home. The best diagnosis they could give me was trigeminal neuralgia, which means severe pain in the head, also known as "suicide disease" because painkillers are ineffective.

They told me I would have to take the steroids for the rest of my life. The drugs did their job and eventually halted the pain. So I stopped taking them for a time, but the pain came back. Instead, I cycled through an on-again, off-again regimen until the pain abated and the bloating from the steroids faded away.

And then Norm came to start his program. To my amazement, he had stopped smoking. His sessions were two or three times a week. At first, he could barely make it through one, accomplishing only five or six minutes of actual training; we spent the rest of the hour focused on recovery.

Over time, he improved and gained strength. While we worked I didn't notice his advances until after about four months, he brought me a porcelain heart with the word "love" printed on it. He dropped it on my desk and said, "Here."

I didn't know how to react.

"Can I take you out for dinner?" he asked.

"I don't date my clients," I said. But deeper down, I had to admit he'd swept me off my feet. He'd put time and effort into this, and that made me feel special. And there he was, standing in front of me looking like a lost puppy.

"Okay," I said. "We can go for dinner. We can go to the Mahle House."

I loved getting dressed up and I adored the Mahle House. I went to some trouble prettying myself up.

After a lovely meal, he drove me home and walked me to the front door. That's where he leaned in and kissed me, and I felt like I wanted to throw up. My body was telling me that this was a dangerous individual, but I talked myself into being nice and being an empath, thinking maybe I was wrong. However, my first intuitive response was on point.

I pulled back and said, "I can't do this with you again."

"Well, I'm just lost for words," he said.

I didn't know what to do. My body was telling me this is a terrible person, and my intellect was saying, ""Maybe you should give this guy a chance."

I slammed the door on him that night. What to do? Later, I went to a psychic who said, "Maybe this man is the right one for you."

The next time I saw Norm, I told him, "It is unethical and inappropriate for me to have anything to do with you. It's against the code of ethics."

He said, "But you can save my life. You can help me regain what my addiction robbed me of."

He knew how to play me. A part of me wanted to care and nurture—to fix the broken.

What I unconsciously knew, but wasn't willing to admit, was that Norm had a lot of my father's characteristics. But he hid those traits well. Like my father, he was a narcissist and a psychopath, but covertly.

We went on weekend trips that were experiences beyond any I had known. He would fly us to the Pan Pacific Hotel in Vancouver where we stayed in suites where rock stars partied. Sometimes it was shopping, where he bought me pretty bangles and clothes, making me feel like Julia Roberts in *Pretty Woman*. He would call room service in the mornings and we would have chocolate-covered strawberries and coffee delivered for breakfast. I was living in a fairy tale and I loved it.

At a deep level, he still repulsed me, but I suppressed it. He was a terrible lover. I suggested Viagra—and he went straight to the doctor to get a prescription. With no clue how to delight a woman, Norm needed instruction—and I delivered. It was pretty easy to discern that his experiences had been mostly with prostitutes. Money provided whatever he wanted.

For a while, the relationship was lovely. I cooked for him while he treated me like a princess, buying me flowers for no reason and spoiling me every chance he got. I had never felt like this before: special, valued, and somehow, that I deserved to have a life that was easy. I don't know anyone who doesn't want that.

Then one day he texted me, saying it was over. He was a businessman, and could not continue. This was the first discard of the cycle of narcissistic abuse.

I had had no warning. One minute he was engaged with me, then nothing.

"I demand an explanation," I said. "You don't get to walk away just like that without telling me what this is about."

He intimated that I'd done something wrong. But I had not. I pressed deeper. "You owe me an explanation," I said. "You pursued me. You did so much to win me over, and now this? You need to explain yourself because I will not accept this."

Yet again, I'd allowed myself to buy into a fantasy, right back into the abuse cycle. I was blind to what must have been obvious to others, unable to figure it all out. What had I done wrong?

A few weeks later, he was back. "I'm so sorry," he said. "I got scared." It was the same old story. I recognized it but lacked the tools to stop it. We repeated that cycle for two years. He would come back, buy me a diamond ring, take me to Mexico—or I would book a time for us to go and, at the last minute, he would sabotage our plans and cancel.

I called him a *fucking idiot*.

"It's your loss," I said. But inside I struggled to understand why he was doing this to me.

I demanded that we see a counsellor and he had to pay. Sometimes he showed up, sometimes not, leaving me with a bill I couldn't afford. Those costs were irrelevant to him. He had inherited about five hundred million dollars from his parents, Jewish immigrants who had invested in Toronto real estate. He had never worried about money. Never had he earned a living.

He often flew back to Toronto, where he still had a wife and kids, buying the children expensive cars—and then he'd come back and tell me what a terrible mother I was because I didn't do the same for my son.

I suggested that we see a new counsellor: Mark Smith of Family Tree Counselling. I had done some work with him earlier on Skype just after I had received my ICBC settlement. He had told me that I would likely fall in love with a psychopath because two psychopaths had raised me.

When he said that, I felt like I'd been kicked in the gut. But sure enough, here I was two years later, loving a psychopath.

Mark scheduled a Skype session with us. We'd hardly begun the hour when Mark said, "You both carry the same baggage. Both your parents are offspring from the Second World War—the trauma of abandonment and abuse is one thing that ties you together. Your parents were abused by their parents and they, in turn abused you. You are wounded children, re-enacting the trauma on each other."

What Mark was saying made sense, and I committed to going through this process with Norm.

To Norm, Mark said, "You've got to have Germana's back. You need to support her." He listed a few things that Norm had to do differently in order for us to have a chance together. I watched Norm turn white and back away from the screen.

"If you don't do these things," Mark said, "this relationship is not worth continuing."

I turned to Norm. "Are you willing to commit to this?"

He crossed his arms. His body language told me that he wanted control—to be the puppeteer.

At our next session, Norm didn't show up. "What should I do?" I asked.

"You need to get into a program for narcissistic/abusive behaviour," Mark said. "This guy has savagely abused you and you can't even see it."

Two days later, after not hearing from Norm, I discovered he had a new girlfriend. How did I know? Pictures of them were all over Facebook, so I messaged him, telling him I felt sorry for her.

"I know what you will do to her," I said. "You're not a better man now. You may be able to con her for a while, but she will be on the receiving end of the rage that you bury so well."

I stayed in therapy, specifically aimed at narcissistic/abusive recovery. I connected the dots of how I was trying to get my unresolved father-daughter needs met through this relationship. In many ways, Norm was better than my father, at least on the surface, but he was just as evil deeper down: unreliable, shaming, blaming, unavailable, and disrespectful—just like my father.

Norm even convinced me once that my father wanted to see me. Piero would call, and Norm would say, "Fathers love their daughters."

"You don't know my dad," I said.

I remember one Christmas when Norm took me to the Pan Pacific; we had set a date to see my father for tea. Two hours before we were to meet, my father phoned. "Don't come. I won't see you today." And he hung up.

I remember Norm shaking his head, looking bewildered.

"That's my father," I said. "He leads me up to these moments. 'I want to see you. Please come'—and then he cancels with no explanation."

And here I was with a man who was no different, attaching myself to a person who had all those damaging, soul-murdering behaviours of transferring all the damage to his victim.

Mark said to me, "Don't go back to Norm. You need to know that he will come back. You break up with these people many times before it all ends. And they never go away. They keep hovering around. You need to break off all contact."

I blocked his cell phone. I blocked him on Facebook and everywhere else I could. Still, he would drive to my house and sit in his car out front—sit there for half an hour or more with his car idling. Sometimes he would come up the walk and start pounding on my front door. I would sit on the other side, shaking.

I fantasized about taking my life. The stress was so huge that the fantasy was with me every day. I didn't know how to feel safe. One of my friends heard me out and said, "You don't want to die—you just want the pain to end."

I needed to hear that.

I called the police. "Please," I said. "Go to his house and tell him to stop." If that didn't work, I thought about having someone go to his house to break his legs.

All this time, he was still seeing the pretty woman with the cute hair. And I had started dating Steve, who was everything Norm wasn't. I'm not saying he was healthy, but he was kind and attentive. One day, I was with Steve in Victoria at the Laurel Point Inn attending a conference, but I was so tired and worn out that I couldn't get out of bed.

I was lying there when I got a text from Norm's girlfriend. She wanted to know about him.

I texted back: "What I know about this man is that he's a covert narcissist and a psychopath. While he was with me, I found out he was also preying on newcomers at Narcotics Anonymous, eliciting blowjobs for money. I didn't know this for a very long time. So he's a sexual predator. He's preying on the weakest and most vulnerable."

"But it all seemed so special," she said.

I told her, "That's all part of the honeymoon phase—part of baiting the trap to make you feel like you've just met the man of your dreams. And you're so enamoured of him that you'll overlook everything else. In fact, you'd ignore his faults even if they came up and slapped you in the face."

I told her we'd been to therapy. I told her he was still married and would not get a divorce. "My guess is that within nine months you'll see some abusive cycles beginning. But in the meantime, please ask him to stop coming to my house because he's bothering me."

For a while, he stopped, and then a few months later, he came back. The stalking didn't end until he sold his house and moved to Vancouver to be close to his girlfriend.

What we'd had, Norm and I, has a name: it's called trauma bonding. I had the same thing with my parents. This was the price I paid for being raised by them.

CHAPTER 7

During all the upheaval in my life, my son was writing his own story. Konrad had been doing drugs for several years and was in a state of full-on psychosis. While living with me, he set my house up for robbery more than once to collect the insurance. Five girls would separately visit his room in a single day. His behaviour was abnormal, and I was enabling him.

At one recovery meeting, I heard a man say that the best thing his parents had ever done for him was to kick him out of the house. But I was afraid my son would die on the street. Instead, he was dying right in front of me.

I lost about $50 000 over a period of a few years because of the effect he had on my home-based business clients. He didn't even have to be there to have a negative impact; the smell of pot permeated the entire house.

I reached a tipping point.

One day, Konrad came home to discover that I had removed the door to his room.

"You're not welcome here," I said. "I love you. I've done everything I can to give you a better life, and you're destroying it right in front of me. If you want to kill yourself, that's on you, but I'm not taking a front-row seat."

Let me backtrack.

A couple of years previously, I was driving over the Malahat when I received a phone call. "Do you know anyone named Konrad Rovinelli?" the voice asked.

"Yes," I said.

"Is he your son?"

"Yes."

"His father, Jack Crowley, has left him a sizable inheritance."

I said, "The man I know as his father is named Ron Belanger."

"Well, Jack Crowley claims that he's your son's father, and he has left half his estate to you and half to his son, but because you weren't married you don't qualify, but your son does."

Apparently, Jack Crowley, alias Ron Belanger, had never completed the proper paperwork on a will and had even spelled my son's name wrong. The executors had been looking for Konrad for at least eight years. Jack/Ron had died in a trailer park somewhere in the United States and had left an informal note expressing his last wishes.

Jack/Ron had had five aliases; when he died he had about $700 000. There was still a two- or three-year process involved to find out if there were any other living progeny belonging to Ron's other aliases, but as soon as Konrad knew that a large sum of money was coming to him, he began using a lot of drugs with money he borrowed from me. He also started selling drugs.

I watched him overdose a few times. Once, he took ketamine, a horse tranquilizer that makes you fall asleep. I said, "You can't do this in my house."

He flew into a rage, grabbed me, and threw me into the wall. He scratched me and shook me. He weighed 200 pounds. I weighed about 130. He could throw me around like a doll.

Luckily, a friend was downstairs painting some rooms and heard the ruckus. She called the police, who removed him. The court put a restraining order on Konrad, denying him access to me or my house.

My son: one more abusive man in my life.

I don't know how it all began or why. I think Konrad was frustrated and angry; and then the drugs. Even before that, I think he felt abandoned, entitled, and rejected.

ADHD prevented him from learning properly in school. He couldn't transfer what was in his head to paper. When he tried to write, it looked like a chicken had danced on the page. I spent thousands of dollars putting him in Kumon and other special programs. I asked the school to allow him to use a computer because that worked. He couldn't write but he was super good on a keyboard.

They wanted to put him on Ritalin, and I said, "Not on your life."

One of my biggest frustrations over the years was with the school system. I remember telling Norm Sutherland, a special mentor, "I only get paid if I meet or exceed my clients' needs. The school system, on the other hand, just rubber-stamps the kids, puts a label on them, and devalues and discards them—they don't care. If I did what you guys did, I wouldn't have a place to live. Shame on you!"

I went to the school board and was eventually blacklisted for speaking up for my son. But I didn't know what else to do. Their answer was Ritalin. My answer to that was "No."

Sure, he might have benefited, but I didn't feel that medicating him was any kind of long-term solution.

Konrad often flipped out; I'd witnessed him punch himself in the face, saying how stupid he was because he couldn't grasp what the other kids were learning. He didn't start reading until he was nine, and the only reason he did then was because he wanted to read the Harry Potter books.

Thank goodness for Harry Potter.

He was in grade seven before they evaluated him and realized that 99.8 percent of people could write and articulate better than he could. By then, I had spent a great deal of time and money trying to determine what was going on.

I'm sure that his early illiteracy was a big contributor to his depression and to every other way he acted out. I remember going to the store once and buying a ton of art supplies. I brought them home and he trashed them in a rage.

Konrad would take his bed apart and sleep under the mattress with a baseball bat and the butcher knives and steak knives from the kitchen. He always left the light on.

His defence mechanisms were so extreme that I didn't know how to get past them. When I saw the baseball bat and the butcher knives in his bedroom, and the art supplies ripped to pieces and scattered on the floor, I actually thought that he might become a serial killer. And in the back of my mind lurked the thought: "Then I might have to kill him because I created him."

I asked him, "What are you afraid of?"

He couldn't answer me. But he lived in such fear and anxiety that I couldn't even get him to take a shower or a bath. No matter what I tried, he fought me every step of the way. I gave up, fearing for my safety. He had converted his fear into rage, and that made him dangerous.

I hired an enneagram coach. "Help me figure out my son because I don't understand what I'm doing wrong," I said

He said, "Ask your son if he's angry or if he's afraid."

When I did, Konrad said, "Mom, I'm afraid—I'm always afraid."

Based on that answer, the coach determined that his enneagram style was a six—the questioner—the most complicated of the styles. They scare themselves by projecting what can go wrong; they're always waiting for the other shoe to drop. Konrad lived his life in defence mode. He also believed that he could never measure up to me—or at least his perception of me.

My life was governed by defence mechanisms from my childhood. I over-compensated. What I showed to the world was a successful individual, and I adopted that image because I wanted my son to have a better life. But what he saw was a hurdle he couldn't leap over, resulting in the opposite effect—the erosion of his self-esteem.

Even as a sad, tortured child, he was an adept manipulator.

"Mom, can we go to Disneyland?"

"No."

"Can I have a trampoline?"

"No."

"Can we have pizza?"

So I ordered pizza, which is what he'd wanted all along.

And yes, we went to Disneyland. He was 11 by the time I could afford it. And you know what? I cried. I had never been there and yes, it really is a happy place.

I suspect that some damage Konrad suffered came from sources linked to my history.

I remember a conversation we had when he was four. Our neighbours across the road had two young girls—they were perhaps five and six. One day they brought him to their house to play.

He returned, bawling. "Mommy," he said. "They put their evil in me."

I inferred that they had sexually assaulted him, and if I was right, they had been abused in their past as well.

Whatever had happened, I couldn't undo it. And I didn't speak to their parents because I knew the history of the family and I was sure that she was a survivor of incest—so those girls and my son had become part of a horrible cycle.

I said to Konrad, "How would you like to get that evil out of your body?" I told him that he was the master of himself;

that he could say no; that he controlled every aspect of his body. He nodded. I hoped those words were enough.

Two amazing support people made a difference to Konrad. I wish they hadn't died so soon.

Norm Sutherland worked with Konrad from the time he entered kindergarten. Norm was an extraordinary man. He worked with the kids who were assigned to a special class. On his fifty-fifth birthday, he took the class camping so that they could connect with nature. He fought for my son's future when nobody else did—when they were ready to throw him away like a piece of trash.

One day, Norm went scuba diving off Snake Island and got the bends. He died on the way up. Two days later, he came to me in a vision, handing me the Olympic torch. "Now it's your turn to carry the torch for your son," he said.

Norm was the one person in the whole system who had cared about my son. There was no other man in Konrad's life—no other man who had his back.

It felt like half the town was at Norm's funeral. Konrad didn't come, but when I told him that Norm had died, he said, "It's okay, mom—he's helping people in heaven now."

After grade school, Konrad when to Nanaimo District Secondary School and was once again placed in a special needs class presided over by Mr. Cole, who was another man with a heart of gold. Konrad got close to him quickly. But when Mr. Cole got sick and started taking antibiotics, he had an adverse reaction. He kept going to the hospital, knowing that something was wrong, but the doctors insisted it was just a flu.

When they discovered that he was having an acute reaction, they airlifted him to the hospital in Victoria, where he died.

Now there was really no one there for my son. He was full of shame, thinking he wasn't good enough or smart enough, and he had no teacher to tell him otherwise. It didn't help that he compared himself to me because I was a super-achiever, over-compensating for the trauma in my life.

Because of how I had been raised, I avoided confrontation. I manipulated to get what I wanted, and I always expected something bad to happen. Most of all, I had constant nightmares that someone would sexually assault my son.

I think Konrad became addicted to drugs because he loathed himself. He told me that he had watched an online video of his girlfriend taking her life. He saw that abused girl hang herself, and I think he hated himself for not helping her.

I didn't know until years later that an older girl had raped him when he was 14. Konrad was sure that she'd become pregnant with his baby, and he felt deep shame and self-hatred for abandoning his child just as he had been abandoned by his father.

Konrad had been in treatment for six months before he told me about the baby. When he did, he said that when he got his inheritance, he was going to rescue that boy.

I told him no. "Konrad, you have no relationship with that boy. He will want nothing to do with you. Even if you are his biological dad, you will appear like a freak to him."

I also warned him that Social Services would come after him for the money that the mother had been getting all those years. She'd had three children by three different fathers. And was that child even Konrad's?

Konrad had kept that secret from the time he was 11 years old. I couldn't imagine the shame he must have felt. There was so much going on with him. He hated me. He hated the fact that I wasn't mothering him the way he needed. Sometimes I bought his approval. And he had huge rage. I got it. I understood.

I often thought that if I had provided him with a stable father who was emotionally available, perhaps those wounds would not have existed. At least, that's the story I told myself. There were times when Konrad acted like he was an adult—taking on the role of equal partner or husband. There were times I had to tell him, "Konrad—I am the mother; you are the child. Stop it!"

And just like that, he would change.

In the end, everything that was going on in our home was too much for him. The line between us snapped, and we each found ourselves on our own.

CHAPTER 8

In 2016, I went to therapy, wanting to understand my relationship with Norm, and wanting to put my life back together. Knowing it was over was a relief, but it left me ripped open.

My time with Norm proved so damaging that it revived every trauma from my childhood. I had wanted to make it work because it gave me so much of what I craved: adventure, intensity, and recognition. I had lied to myself about who he was, pretending that he was "the one." He had sensed that and exploited it, going so far as buying a motorcycle identical to mine even though he didn't ride.

For him, I was just an object to dominate and control. For my part, I believed he loved me. When we were still just dating and I found out that he was married, he pulled out his phone right there in the middle of the street, called his lawyer, and made a big show of telling him to get the paperwork for the divorce done.

It was bullshit. But he did it because he wanted me to have confidence in him. Whenever a red flag appeared, I would look the other way, talking myself out of the obvious.

When he left, I struggled to sleep for months. I avoided people, both socially and intimately.

As I got stronger, I committed to getting back "out there." Maybe it was too soon, but I needed that connection—a desire that probably went all the way back to my childhood. I registered at an online dating site and met Steve, a musician who lived in Vancouver. I felt tentative—unsure if I should be doing this, but I wanted to try. I was blunt and honest with him about my state of heart and mind; I told him I was a mess. It didn't faze him, and he drove over to the island in his truck to meet me. He brought me a giant bouquet, took me out for lunch, and held my hand as we talked. To my surprise, it was a pleasant conversation.

We walked, indulged in a side-by-side pedicure, and he returned home. One mark on the plus side of the Steve register: he also rode a motorcycle. He told me he'd sold songs to Hollywood. I think he was trying to wow me.

"You don't need to try to impress me," I said.

He, too, had suffered a recent wound to his heart. His partner of years had told him that their relationship was done. She had found someone else. "I need someone to validate that I'm still okay," he said.

I replied, "If you want to be with me, you're really sick. Because I'm sick."

We started dating and he would spend too much money on me—money he didn't have. I think he was trying to be what Norm couldn't be.

We dated for five months before we were intimate, and it wasn't good. I kept getting urinary tract infections.

One of his faults was doing for others. I told him, "You're so busy fixing things for others that you don't take care of yourself. You put yourself last in line."

He didn't like that. I suspect he was trying to earn his way into my life. I told him, "You will never live with me. Don't bring your things here and don't leave things in my house. That's a hard boundary. If we were to ever live together, it would be our home, not my home—and I don't want that."

One day, I noticed a bunch of his stuff in the garage and in my closet. "Steve—I specifically said not to do this. You're bringing your things here, and you're doing it behind my back."

He gave me no explanation. And the next thing I knew, he bought me a car. He earned good money, but he didn't own anything. He wouldn't even bring me to his apartment in Vancouver—wouldn't even tell me where it was because he knew I would judge him for it.

When he said he would buy me a car, I thought he was crazy. But he kept talking about it so I said, "I wouldn't mind a used Subaru—that would be great."

He bought me a $120 000, 700 horsepower, Dodge Hellcat. A race car. Brand new.

Saying I was stunned is an understatement.

"You're too sexy to be driving a Subaru," he said.

He wanted to be the big man—the man who could afford toys like this. He couldn't.

"Steve—don't do this!" I said. "This is insane. The payments on this car are like my mortgage payment."

I spent several days telling him "no."

He insisted it was mine.

I didn't know what he was thinking. Maybe if he bought me the car, he would get the girl?

"The vagina doesn't come with the car," I said. I'd already told him I was not ready to commit to him or to anyone. I was still healing.

But that didn't seem to matter. Steve had a shaky sense of boundaries. I told him that I worked all week, and he was welcome on weekends. "Let's do something together," I said. "But I don't want to stay at my house. I live here and work here. I need to get out."

He didn't listen. He would come and just hang out at the house, thinking that was a good time.

"Steve, I specifically said, I don't want to hang out here."

Once we left town and checked into a hotel—and they declined his credit card. So I paid for it. Why was the credit card declined? There were big gaps in what I knew about him.

One day he said, "I'm going to take you to Paris." He bought the tickets. A few weeks before the trip, we rode out to Keremeos for a Sober Riders event.

It's a long ride out to Keremeos, and we would arrive late. Steve had not had the sense to reserve a room for us. By one a.m. I was getting the sense that we might end up sleeping on someone's lawn. And, as expected, Keremeos had no rooms. We kept riding. It annoyed the hell out of me. My inner voice was saying, "If I meant something to you, you would have thought this through and prepared for this trip. If you can't do that here, how can I trust you in Europe?"

We rode for hours until we reached a tiny village where we got a horrible little dirty room because that was all that was available.

The next morning, we rode back to Keremeos and all day he was right there, clinging to me like a baby koala. He followed me everywhere, shadowing my steps. "Do you want water? Do you want something to eat?"

At the end of the day, I said, "I won't ever do that with you again. I felt like you didn't let me just be me. You were constantly shadowing me. You didn't let me socialize on my own."

"But I didn't know anyone there," he said.

"Well, I only knew three of them myself. These are just people who stopped doing drugs and alcohol and are creating a fresh life."

I was ashamed by his behaviour—and uncomfortable.

The trip to Europe was fast approaching. I had my Jazzercise classes covered, willing to take the financial loss for the month.

Meanwhile, each weekend he arrived on the island later. He wouldn't arrive on a Saturday until five or six p.m. and, often, I was on my way out by then. I told him that if his life was so dysfunctional that he couldn't get here until five or six on a Saturday night, then he couldn't expect me to be waiting for him.

That got his back up.

"Look," I said. "I'm not getting my needs met. You're not capable of hearing me or matching me."

He shrugged, assuming I would change my mind. He was mistaken. I had never fallen in love with him, although I empathized, recognizing that he was damaged. I thought I might be able to help him, so I arranged a Skype session for Steve with Mark, a respected therapist.

On the day of the appointment, I set Steve up in my bedroom with my computer while I worked with a client downstairs. When I came back upstairs after my appointment, I asked him, "How did the session go?"

"What session?" he asked.

I looked at him.

"Oh—I fell asleep."

I was livid. "Mark made a special agreement with me to see you, and you blew that off? You knew that the reason you were here was to see him. If you're not willing to work on yourself, we have no relationship."

But still—our trip was approaching. I had an unsettling feeling that he would propose to me in Paris.

I had so many misgivings that I saw a psychic. She said, "I don't see the money part lasting. He's done terrible things. There are issues." She was careful to not be too specific, but she dropped enough hints that my radar went up even more. This was not good.

The car was also causing me more grief every day. Driving it cost nine hundred dollars a month. I couldn't afford the gas or the insurance.

You put me in a bad financial position," I told him. "I can't afford to keep this car. Unless you can see your way to giving me an extra thousand dollars a month to cover the costs, this isn't working."

I suspected that he was trying to make me indebted to him so that I would have to accept him in my life, if only to pay for the car. I became more angry because I felt that he had taken advantage of me.

One week before our flight to Paris, the girl who I had entrusted to take over my classes and who had apprenticed under me to become a Jazzercise instructor, resigned and took the other instructors with her to open her own studio. She planned to take over my clients, assuming that I was leaving and wouldn't be able to fight back.

What I didn't know at the time was that she had been orchestrating this meticulously for six months. I confronted the other instructors; they had all been drinking this girl's Kool-Aid. She was just another narcissist/sociopath who was bent on destroying me. Her husband was wealthy—he had tried to buy my business at one point. But when he told me the price he was willing to pay, I told him. "First, I didn't create this in order to sell it, and secondly, that offer is an insult to my intelligence."

Instead, they had planned to steal the business from me—and that would be easy because I wouldn't be in the country.

They hadn't bargained on my anger or determination. "I won't be going anywhere," I said. "And I'll be teaching all the classes."

They would not take away my career.

I cancelled the trip and taught all the Jazzercise classes. In a way, I felt a huge sense of relief. This had turned out to be the best excuse not to go to Paris with Steve. Within two weeks, the two other instructors realized they had been conned. One of them apologized. I understood and forgave her, knowing firsthand what it was like to be duped.

Ironically, the woman's husband was my financial adviser. I reported him for trying to buy my business for his wife while representing me. That report went on his professional file.

But she wasn't through yet. She tried to smear me in front of the regional manager with lies. But the regional manager had other ideas. She said, "You need to keep your husband away for all these affairs and dealings. If you do this ever again, I will permanently take your licence away."

I was so done. Here was this couple, trying to destroy my business—trying to destroy me. And here we go again! Norm had tried to destroy me too.

CHAPTER 9

All this time, I was prepping, training, and participating in a bodybuilding show. At this point, I needed to focus on me. I had changed myself so much trying to be what I thought Norm wanted—and what all the other men in my life had expected—I needed to reconnect with my authentic self.

The questions I posed were, "What does Germana need? What does Germana want?"

My long-time sponsor, Val, said, "Germana, you said that when you turn 50, you want to compete one more time. This matters to you. Why have you not done this yet?"

I was 51. But damn it—she'd said it and it was true—I had made that vow. So I talked to the president of the British Columbia Body Building Association and asked him, "Who do you recommend as a trainer?"

He gave me the name of Alan Dyck, who lived in Kelowna. Alan charged me $700 to take me on an as a client. All our sessions were by satellite. He sent me the menu and texted me every morning. How much did I weigh? What kind of shape was I in? How was I feeling? I followed a stringent routine for nine weeks before the big Vancouver regional show.

This was my way of saying, "Hey—I'm still alive and kicking!"

I won the award for Overall Best Poser, first in my division, and first in three other categories. I got so many trophies and so much swag that I couldn't even get it all to the car in one trip.

I felt like a million bucks. I won the show—everything I entered. The photos were sensational. I looked great—and pretty.

After that, I had one goal in mind: the Nationals in Toronto. I went back to Alan's gruelling training routine. But he was dieting me so light that it recalled how I had felt when I was abused. That feeling was solidified when he didn't show up in Toronto after he'd promised to be there with the team.

He was paying a lot more attention to another woman he had trained.

Me? I was over-trained and ill-prepared.

I got second in Canada as a natural physique athlete competing against women more than ten years my junior.

Still, despite training so hard, dieting so strenuously, and working with such dedication, I had not achieved what I wanted to. Alan's method of training felt cruel. Still, I did my best. But when I saw my pictures from the competition, I wanted to throttle him. I didn't look right.

When I got home, he sent me another bill for $400, assuming I would stick it out with him. He told me he would get me to the next level, start me on steroids, and show me how to block the evidence from the screening tests, assuring me I wouldn't get caught.

That went against my principles. It would be like screwing my best friend's husband and pretending I hadn't. If I started taking steroids, I guessed I would start drinking again. I would hate myself. There was no integrity in that; I'd be cheating. And besides, I could get caught.

The $400-bill was for a reverse diet that he said I needed to avoid ballooning up into a giant monster now that I wasn't starving myself on the training diet.

I sent the diet back, explaining that he had no integrity in charging me for it. Of all the bills I had received, this was too much.

Chris, a trainer I had met at the Toronto show a member of the International Federation of Body Builders, grabbed my interest. He'd had a team of athletes at the show who he strongly supported. They had team shirts and jackets and did well, often netting firsts, seconds, and thirds.

One woman, Shirley Mattieu, was from Victoria. At the time, she was 51—a bikini athlete originally from South Africa. She was poised, distinguished, and exhibited a beautiful personality. She was also drop-dead hot. She told me she had been at the same show the year before with a different trainer, but after observing Chris, she hired him.

I had watched her compete. She took home second of 36 women in the open division, which meant that she was up against all the women, most much younger.

I thought, *Whoever is working with you is doing an excellent job.* I was so impressed that a woman could look that good in her fifties. Looking at her, watching her, I realized there was something here that I wanted to understand.

I called Chris and we had a brief consultation. I asked if he still accepted new athletes. He said, "You need to tell your trainer that you're leaving him before I will accept you. I don't want him to think that I'm head-hunting athletes at shows."

His integrity impressed me. I sent Alan a note telling him that I would no longer be requiring his services. "I think you've taken me as far as you can, and I thank you for all that you taught me."

Then I hired Chris. He used a digital program called Elite Pro that allows you to upload your photos, your measurements, and your weight. Chris then designed a program based on my statistics. Building on that information and our discussions, he would send me my program, and we would Skype twice a month for an hour.

Chris' model differed vastly from anything I had done. Where once I'd had egg whites and chicken breast, I was now eating filet mignon for breakfast as well as whole eggs and other high-protein foods.

Chris said I had to build up my legs—the weakest part of my body. I told him that I'd had a spinal cord injury, which was likely the reason that the bottom half of my body didn't match the top half.

He asked me to consider taking SARMS, a class of therapeutic compounds that have similar properties to anabolic agents, but with reduced androgenic properties. SARMS has the advantage of androgen-receptor specificity, tissue selectivity, along with the lack of steroid-related side effects. In the United States and Europe, SARMS is considered a type of modern medicine to deal with various physical conditions.

Before jumping in and buying them, I asked Shirley, another athlete, if she had taken them. She had. "Do whatever Chris tells you to do," she said.

Chris explained that at my age, my body would not release growth hormones or testosterone. I was at a different stage of the life cycle. I thought, too, about the athletes I'd seen at the show—the ones he trained. They were outstanding. So I bought the SARMS and started taking them.

The weird neuropathy in my body disappeared; my tendon pain and fatigue vanished. I had more energy, vitality, and spunk. I felt like a 30-year-old.

On the downside, my body developed muscles I wasn't used to, and that made me uncomfortable. It upset me because I wanted to feel sexy and these muscles were having the opposite effect. I wasn't used to the density. I gained 12 pounds and none of it was fat; I was just bigger.

I told Chris how much I didn't like it and also asked him about the women in their fifties and sixties that I was seeing. "How do they look so good?" I asked. They weren't having plastic surgery.

He told me about polypeptides, which are chains of amino acids. They reset your telomeres, which are an essential part of human cells that affect how our cells age. In effect, telomeres are caps at the end of each strand of DNA that protect our chromosomes, like the plastic tips at the end of shoelaces.

He told me to buy the polypeptides, take them for three months, wait three weeks, and then start taking them again. He told me that my genes would reset—my body would feel 10 or 15 years younger on the inside. When I investigated, I read about doctors saying that this was the medicine of the future.

I thought, "What have I got to lose? I'm on the downhill slide of my life. My son is an adult now. So why not?" As a bonus, polypeptides also make your hair and nails grow and your skin glow.

I had a spinal court injury and a thyroid injury; my pituitary and adrenal glands were damaged—all because of stress from trauma and from being raised in a hostile environment.

So I bought some. I noticed an immediate change. I was glowing like a woman does when she's pregnant. People were saying, "Wow! You look good!" My hair grew longer than it ever had, and my body was behaving like one much younger.

I was floored. I asked Chris, "Why don't other trainers tell you about this?"

"Because they're trying to sell you steroids," he said.

"I don't want to take steroids," I said. "I'm scared of steroids."

If I got nothing else out of my relationship with Chris—I got that, and it was worth it. I developed the most amazing ass I'd ever owned. It grew out by an inch. My legs were never quite as big as he wanted them, but oh my ass! I realized it one day when I was trying to put on my tights and I was sure I had them on backwards, but I looked at the tag. "They're not backwards! My ass grew!"

And it wasn't fat—it was muscle. Chris said we had to build up my quads to match the back end. I said, "The only way my quads are going to grow bigger now is if I staple a steak to them!"

He scheduled me to compete in Vancouver with the Canadian Body Building Federation. But Chris' wife had just competed with the international arm of the federation in China and had won fifth place in the world in her division. He said that the way they had treated her was so disappointing that he would rather I didn't compete in Vancouver. In retrospect, I should have said, "No—I've qualified, and I'm going."

But I wanted his approval, so I pulled out and instead, registered with the Canadian Physique Alliance. I was scheduled for shows in Vancouver, Toronto, and Pittsburgh.

I started at the regionals in Vancouver and won the entire show: five trophies. I was pleased—beyond pleased, winning other prizes along with the trophies. But I wasn't as thrilled as I deserved to be, still uncomfortable with my body. It didn't feel quite right to me. It felt somehow watery. And this was the issue in my relationship with Chris. I wasn't sure if he couldn't see me or if he didn't have enough measurements or if I intimidated him. Another athlete had told me that intimidation was the issue—maybe and maybe not—but something wasn't right.

When I saw my pictures, I wasn't happy. I still saw my body as too watery, too thick, and too bulky.

WE DO RECOVER

A few weeks later, I went to the next level: the Toronto show. At the time, I didn't know that I was suffering from a urinary tract infection. I was drinking so much water that the test came back negative. Still, my immune system was compromised. I could tell something was going on because my urine smelled sweet—as though I was diabetic, and I wasn't eating any sugar, so it made little sense.

I visited a naturopath and told her that I was having a hard time sleeping, and sleep was important. If you don't sleep, your body doesn't recover. She told me to take U-Dream, a supplement I could buy at the Health Food Store. So there I was taking a mountain of supplements in the morning and more during the day. My kitchen counter looked like a pharmacy. I didn't know that one of the effects of U-Dream is that it can cause people to eat during the night without remembering—and that had already been an issue for me years ago.

Some mornings I would wake up to find tiny bits of chocolate chip rice cakes in the bed with me. I panicked. My system was backfiring. I wasn't being congruent. But I'd made a commitment, and one way or another, I would see it through.

Meanwhile, Chris was stroking my ego—told me I could become pro—that he saw an enormous future for me. And I bought into it. Yes, I was muscular; I had a good body; my waist was too thick, but still . . .

I did everything I was supposed to do. I had sponsors. I was looking great.

Then we were off to Toronto. They placed me in the 35 years and over division. That made it a unique animal. I looked the competition over. It was clear that at least 65 percent were on steroids. Their asses were striated, and women don't get that unless they're taking something.

Several women in the show were Chris' athletes. And they were small—like little ballerinas, shredded to the bone. Out of 14 competitors, I placed sixth. I was watery and I didn't look right and I knew it. I didn't want anyone to show me the video, and I didn't want to see the pictures.

In Toronto, I shared a room with a woman called Katie Una, a 58-year-old bikini athlete. She was gorgeous—like Joan Collins in *Dallas*. She wasn't just beautiful; she was also sweet and kind. She too didn't do as well as she had wanted. Still, she was 58 going up against 35-year-olds. We developed a friendship. I talked about going to Pittsburgh. Should I keep going? Should I finish this? I had already paid for my ticket.

I went. Chris came to my room in Pittsburgh to wish me luck, and as he was leaving, he said, "I'll see you on stage."

"I've already been up," I said.

He had so much going on, he didn't even realize that I'd already finished.

"I didn't place," I said.

"What?"

I told him what I'd seen and heard backstage. The women were talking openly about the steroids they were taking—how big a difference it made. And if you looked, you could see it in their faces. Their structure was altered, their noses protruded, and their voices were deeper. Some were developing Adam's apples.

I'd heard one woman say, "Yeah—you've just got to find the right trainer, and he'll give you the good stuff."

I didn't know what to make of it. I looked at their features and thought, *I don't want to look like you.*

It was all falling into place for me after Toronto, where we'd been in a room, stripped down naked to get our spray tans. One young girl was standing looking at the wall and turned slowly towards me. Between her legs was a clitoris that looked like a West Coast slug. That's what steroids will do: grow the clitoris like a penis. And the trainers will tell these women, "The only way you'll be able to compete is to take this stuff."

By then, you're often in so far, that you keep going. And there are a lot of young women who will do anything to have that look: that lean, muscular body. I realized that there is an entire culture of trainers that target women—and men—who have a body image disorder or have a need for acknowledgement or recognition. They need to look a certain way. The trainer manipulates them and gets them into programs that are riddled with drugs—and riddled in a way that deforms and disfigures people's bodies. And this stuff can kill you if you don't know what you're doing.

There was one trainer at the Toronto show with dozens of athletes. He donated $50 000 to the promoter, telling him how many pro cards he wanted—and he got them. This man would only accept an athlete if they made a 12-month commitment and paid $1 200 a month. And they had to be on a drug cycle for two months before he would even see them.

The Toronto show was promoted as a tested show, but it was rife with people on steroids.

It opened my eyes to the industry: so full of narcissism and ego and mental sickness. These were people looking for approval from strangers they would never see again. They were disfiguring their bodies, abandoning their families, and sacrificing their personal relationships to have a single shot at fame or shame, depending on what happened on that stage.

I understood one thing: this was not why I was doing this.

I looked at my photos from Pittsburgh. Some looked good, but my belly was distended and bloated. What was that? How had that happened? I had never seen my body do that.

I returned home. The plane ride was the best part of that trip. I was sitting next to a woman, Caroline Stocks, who had just written a book, *Elephants Before Unicorns*, meant to inspire and educate women. She turned to me and said she couldn't help but notice my bum. She told me she had a hard time getting herself motivated to go to the gym.

I told her, "I encourage people to think of it as a time of fun for their little girl."

No one had explained it to her that way. She told me that she had been adopted and suffered abandonment issues along with a host of other problems.

I said, "Just because your parents abandoned you doesn't mean you will keep on abandoning you. Your needs are important. You won't survive by taking care of everyone's needs but your own. Your body is your temple."

She hired me on the spot, and I still train her today. But while we were talking, she told me, "You need to write a book!"

And so I did.

You never know how God will show up in your life and how you will end up being of service.

When I got back home, I realized my trainer was subtly encouraging me to take steroids for my next competition. He didn't come right out and say it, but I felt like I was being groomed. I was so disappointed in him.

He had put me on a platform to compete against women who were taking an enormous amount of drugs. It was like being asked to compete in a boxing ring with one arm tied behind your back.

Chris wanted to keep me on. I was a low maintenance athlete. I didn't cause trouble, wasn't an emotional wreck, and I did as I was told. I was honest, straightforward, and reliable, and I paid my bills.

I said to him, "Please cancel my agreement with you. Even if you send me a menu, I won't follow it. I need a break. I've done two years of hard training and hard competing and I'm not happy with the body I'm living in. It's too big. I don't feel like a beautiful, sexy woman."

He was kind about it. But I still felt like he had set me up, and I had some grieving to do. If I'd stuck to my original plan to compete in that one show in Vancouver—which was all I wanted—I probably would not have been competing against drug-abusing athletes.

I had betrayed and abandoned myself again. I'd been looking for approval. I announced on Facebook that I was done competing because the name of the game was drugs, but I also said that I was proud of myself and grateful to my trainer.

The naked truth was that when I came home, I considered taking the drugs.

"Maybe that's all I have to do, and I'll reach my goals."

I talked to Val, my sponsor, and she said, "Germana, can you hear what you're saying? That stuff changes you."

Her words stopped me cold. But I'd been drinking that Kool-Aid, and I realized, that's how it happens. You want to be accepted. You want that goal. For me, it was about wanting to hold on to my youth—about not accepting my age, which was a huge hook for me. I never wanted to grow old. Being old and not being able to look after myself were two of my greatest fears. I'm a bit of a narcissist in some areas. Validation is one of my driving needs. And I want intensity. On that stage, I got it all.

I also have a fear of rejection, and I have anxiety, so it's a perfect storm for something to turn out terrible for me.

Figuring out how to establish a more integral relationship with myself became key. After talking to Val, I agreed, "I'm not going to do that. That's not who I am. That's not my life's work, and that's not my soul's purpose. I don't want that lifestyle."

Physical problems plagued me too. My gut hurt. One morning, I woke up sobbing, my innards in excruciating pain.

My doctor ran a gamut of tests and phoned me within hours. "You have a kidney infection and a bladder infection."

"But they tested me for a urinary tract infection a few weeks ago!" I said.

"Yes. But you were tested at one of the labs that doesn't do good tests."

My immune system was in awful shape. My lower abdomen was distended. I couldn't pass enough water. I filled the doctor's prescription and after taking the pills for a while, my body returned to normal. Through that, I understood that I wasn't meant to do this. My true heart and soul work was spiritual. Some of that work is couched in fitness, and some of it manifests as hypnotherapy. All of those pieces come together. My work is about elevating people to love themselves and care for themselves. I want to help people blossom—that's what makes my life meaningful. The whole bodybuilding piece was about trying to prove that I was not a wreck at 53 years old.

I made new decisions. One was about staying as active as I could. Every day, I do an extra hour of cardio to offset my metabolism because I like food. At one point, I was 180 pounds, and that was fat. It worried me that once I let go of the discipline and rigidity of training, I would balloon. Fears of being rejected for not playing the role of the super athlete played a huge part in my life. Part of my identity was all tied up with that.

As a bodybuilder, when I met potential partners, I would show them parts of my body, accompanied with a warning: "Don't freak out about the size of this or that—I'm training for a show. I'm an athlete, and I won't always look like this. This is not forever. This is a small chapter of my life."

So here I was, terrified of not being good enough and realizing how I had tied that level of hyper-rigidity into my unkindness towards myself, telling myself it was for my own good. That reflected my childhood, when others had been unkind towards me. I had taken on that hostile parenting role with myself. Part of me was fine with that because it modelled what I had grown up with: no time for fun—just get on with it. I reflected an abusive relationship, but I was my own bully.

I needed to set myself free. I needed to be a little feminine girl again. I needed to have love and compassion for the part of me that felt inadequate—that believed I had to do these grandiose things—all for a little love and approval.

So there it was: the dismantling of this persona and this rigidity and the restrictions and the discipline. I had to weave a new tapestry.

I refused to weigh myself—that was one of the things that had to go. "I will not let a scale or a number tell me if I'm enough—or if I'm good enough. It will only make me crazy. I'm already prone to it—I don't need any help with that."

The one thing I did put on my schedule was the daily cardio to allow my body to metabolize the muscle I had built up. I practised daily self-care: prayer, meditation, appreciation, a gratitude list, journaling, and when there was time between clients—listening to inspirational podcasts.

It took more than three months for me to get my body back to the point where I could look at it naked and feel good.

In December 2018, I listened to Michael Mirdad, a spiritual teacher, who draws from *A Course in Miracles*. I wanted to get God into my life. Mirdad had a beautiful take on the *Twelve Days of Christmas* that centred around saying goodbye to the negative qualities that you embody from all the signs of the Zodiac—and then building up the positive qualities. He explained it wasn't just about building up the positive—you also get to say goodbye and forgive and let go of all the things from the past year to get ready for the New Year.

You write it all down and then burn the list.

I wrote the names of all the toxic people in my life and my toxic relationships, and that I wanted to love and be loved. I burned the paper. I noticed that the most toxic relationship I had was with myself—and I transferred that on to other people and tried to make it about them.

I recognized that Mirdad was a true healer and a true teacher. He wasn't all about himself. He was not about ego. Thanks to him and to the work I did, I could recognize men who walked into my life who were toxic—and I wasn't having any of that.

Not now—not ever again.

CHAPTER 10

As I entered a new place in my life, I asked myself, "Who are you? What are you committed to? What is the purpose of this life? What are the lessons that you need to learn?"

The answers had nothing to do with seeking the approval of strangers. They were not about finding validation outside of myself.

What was my soul agreement for this lifetime? That was the question I needed to answer. As I pondered these questions, I realized the answers lay in teaching spiritual principles and engaging in therapeutic practices that were also spiritual and grounded in undeniable truths. I wanted to support people to endure less pain and suffering—to assist them in removing the veils in front of their eyes so they could see their self-inflicted harm and their self-imposed suffering, just as I had. I wanted to lead them back to loving themselves and help them create a purposeful and meaningful life.

This was my hope. This was where I belonged. I might do this work in the guise of fitness training or talk therapy or nutrition or hypnotic therapy, but this was my calling. Years before, when I'd explored what my emotional child yearned to do, the answer had been simple: to teach people how to love themselves.

Now, as an adult, I realized that if we relied on our bodies to prove that we were good enough, we would never feel adequate. The body doesn't live forever. It grows old and dies.

I clarified for myself where to invest my energy in this next chapter of my life, and what resonated strongly with me was teaching compassion and forgiveness, and letting others know that we are all loved and cared for if we allow it.

An important part of this work was decoding the distorted thinking others had ingrained in me throughout my childhood. I could finally step back, look at my programming and recognize that it was unhealthy. To a large extent, my past had propelled me through my life. I came from an unhealthy family fuelled by addiction and mental illness. I recall a sentence in a book about adult children of alcoholics: *"The thought never dawned on us that we carried this disease in the form of persistent fear and distorted thinking. This is para-alcoholism as we know it."*

My need for stability and validation influenced and directed a lot of my behaviours. I worked to get those needs met by trying to do what others expected of me and hoped that if I did the right thing people would love me. I abandoned myself repeatedly, not understanding that this little inner munchkin that needed fixing was so broken that it was robbing me of my true power.

This realization crept in—slipped in under the door when I wasn't looking until one day I saw it: I was raised by people who were crazy, so I was going to be crazy no matter how hard I tried to be otherwise. You can't come out of that kind of a dysfunctional childhood without some twisted ideas about your value.

I had created a perfect theatrical piece with my bodybuilding competition. I'd had multiple reasons for diving in, and one of them was my age. I was afraid of being overlooked and of being unattractive—all my fears about getting older were on stage; I was trying not only to control them, but also to reverse the very process of aging. As I came up against the reality of bodybuilding, I saw that things don't happen to you; they happen for you. How was I going to turn this disappointment or this defeat or this anger into a gift?

I was either going to stay in a place of telling myself that I was a stupid idiot who invested years and thousands of dollars doing this or I was going to ask myself, "Who am I?" I listened to the answer:

"I'm an athlete. No one can take that away from me. Even if I don't want to compete and no longer do what the sport demands, I remain an athlete."

The sport required too much. Still, it gave me something valuable. But I never felt that I had much value unless I was caring for others.

This was the one way I had of breaking that pattern. I bought food and prepared it—I shopped and prepped and created a structure that I had never had. I mothered and nurtured myself. That was one part. Another part told me, "Just get your ass to the gym and train." I became both the nurturing parent and the militant parent—the one who told me that no matter what I did, it was never enough.

So for whom was I doing all this? What did I get out of it? It surprised me that I felt repulsed by what I had experienced as a competitor, and how I was so locked into believing that this one moment—this one win—would make everything better. It was like an addiction of a different kind. I wanted that one hit—that one glass of wine—that one orgasm. I was looking for love or meaning or self in all the wrong places.

This was my "a-ha" moment—my spiritual breakthrough. I was proud of telling my trainer that I would not follow any program he gave me. That whole experience pushed me into a different direction—not the one I was destined for.

And now, after it was all over, I was uncomfortable in my body. I had disfigured it. A year after quitting, I was still coming back to what I believed was my natural, healthy body. I refused to weigh myself. I needed time to recreate a tender, soft, compassionate relationship with myself. I had to learn to have better boundaries; I had to learn how to speak up and ask for I what I needed and wanted. I'd been using bodybuilding as my excuse to set a boundary, not understanding that boundaries are inherent.

I had learned to get my needs met by using excuses. I had found things that made me busy, and when I was busy, I had a reason to keep people away.

I grieved my body. My torso, my legs, my arms, and shoulders were all bigger than I was comfortable with.

I'd spent two years building them. I now knew that as I approached my body differently, it would change and become what was natural for me.

I had to be kind to myself in this place. I had accomplished something, but I had carried those good things too far. I had gone to a place of wanting to be a superhero. "Yay! I'm 53! I will climb Everest. Without oxygen! Backwards! Watch me go!"

I was looking for other people's validation. Maybe this new trainer—maybe he could take me to the top. And I still had those fleeting moments of thinking, "Maybe a new trainer . . ." But I promised myself: "No. I will never do that again."

If I had to weigh one more piece of chicken, I would explode. I could eat healthy food without becoming a petri-dish experiment.

The end of this phase of my life was intensely spiritual for me. I came back to the wild woman and healer that I was. The wounded healer is an archetype that is me. I had experienced enough—carried enough scars, that I could see those wounds in others. They can't hide and they can't BS me. I'd been to that dance. I understood the pain of others. And I knew to ask, "What do you want to do about it?"

CHAPTER 11

In 2018, Brad came into my life.

I met him on a dating site. We had our profiles up, both of us with our motorcycles. We sent a few messages back and forth and one of us said, "I'd love to ride with you sometime." And that was it—just one more chat on a dating site.

About a year later, I received a friend request from him on Facebook. I asked him, "How do I know you?" He reminded me about our online chat and that we had mutual friends. All right. I granted his request.

A year later, on April 27, 2019, he sent a meme about healing and recovery. That's when I sat back and took notice. I scouted his page and had a good look at his photo. He was darn handsome. In fact, super handsome: leaning against his bike, big smile, silver fox hair, good body . . .

"You're easy on the eyes," I messaged him. "But according to your bio, you live in Terrace!"

"No," he messaged back. "I'm from Terrace, but I live in Nanaimo."

"Really? That's exciting."

"Yeah—I just went for a ride with two of your friends."

It was a Friday afternoon. "Would you like to meet for a tea on Sunday?"

"Yes."

We arrived at Starbucks at about the same time. And we couldn't stop grinning at each other. We were like little kids or like the cat that ate the biggest, fattest canary known to man. I felt safe and comfortable with Brad. He seemed relaxed with me. I didn't ask him about his financial status. He'd dated enough women whose first question was often, "What's your net worth?"

I was clear with him. "I don't give a shit how much money you make. I'm looking for someone to share my life with. If I need you to make a certain amount of money to be in my life, then my motives are suspect and I'm not going to attract the right person."

We'd been sipping tea and grinning at each other for a while when I said, "Do you want to go for lunch at Cuckoo's in Coombs?"

We rode our motorcycles side by side down the highway, still grinning at each other—and even without the grins, riding side by side is sexy.

Our Cheshire-cat smiles lasted right through lunch. We discovered all the things we had in common. Brad was also in recovery and in fact, his sponsor was someone I had known for more than 20 years. Lunch wasn't long enough. We rode back to my house—and I never brought people home.

We sat on the back deck and drank water and talked and talked. I knew right then—or maybe as far back as Starbucks: I would marry this man.

I had my home group that night, so I said goodbye. But over the next few days, we texted, chatted, and saw each other as much as possible. What I didn't know then was that he had already told his mother and his sister that he was madly in love.

The feeling was entirely mutual. Brad was my dream guy, embodying all the qualities that had been on my wish list: he was into fitness and healthy food, rode a motorcycle, was in recovery, was emotionally intelligent, and was capable of genuine heartfelt conversations.

I had told him in our first deep conversation on that day we met that I believed that the reason we select a partner is to help each other heal childhood wounds. We either do that consciously or we rip each other apart.

I said, "I've had enough ripping and I've had enough damage. I have hurt enough, and I don't need any more. Do you understand that? Do you understand what that means?"

We had almost identical childhood wounds. His mother was abusive, dehumanizing, and cruel—like my father, who was crueller, but the wounding was the same.

Brad said, "I understand. I've had enough crazy. I've been single for 10 years and I'm ready to have integrity in a relationship and to understand the purpose of it. I want this to last for the next 30 years. I will not fuck this up. In fact, we're not having sex."

That impressed me and endeared him to me. He had no interest in only my body or in parading me around like a trophy girlfriend. We spent a lot of time talking, connecting, and being honest with each other. Transparency: what a pleasant change.

I even told a couple of clients, "I have a funny feeling about this one. This is the guy for me." But I also hedged my bets. "I might be wrong, and I'm okay with that. I'm allowed to be wrong. But I'm pretty sure this is it."

Brad had been working on ships—captaining tugboats and other vessels—and had recently completed a nine-month course to upgrade his skills. The final test took place out of town a little more than a week after we had connected.

He mentioned that the timing was perfect. Before upgrading, he stayed on the ships as long as possible to get the biggest paycheque—often weeks or months at a time. I told I would not be in a relationship with someone who was never around. We made an agreement that he would work one week on and one week off.

When he came back with his certification and got a terrific job with union benefits, we changed our agreement to two weeks on and two weeks off for the additional money. The difference was appreciable. But I was clear when I told him, "If you make it more than two weeks, I'm out. I can't do that. In my mind, if you do that, you're a workaholic—and I'm being abandoned. That's my core issue."

Even with him being away for two weeks, my issues were triggered. I recognized them, but the grief was still there. I didn't put it on him, but a part of me believed he was not coming back. And I told him: "I know that you tell me that you're coming back. The little girl inside me doesn't believe you."

My insecurity about not being good enough kicked in, the dark side telling me I had to be bigger and better so he would accept me. When I finished competing in bodybuilding, I was convinced he would run away. The expectation that I would be rejected was so all-consuming that I would have panic attacks. And the voice telling me, "I'm going to get fat now; I'm going to have cellulite on my ass; I'm going to have a tubby tummy."

I thought I had to be super-Germana and now I wasn't anymore. I wasn't enough.

The only thing that helped was digging back into the materials from Adult Children of Alcoholics and my 12-step programs. They helped me to stop obsessing with Brad and his feelings about me and instead, to focus on me. *I'm me and I'm enough. And if I'm not enough for you, it's okay. I'm okay. I don't need your stamp of approval.*

I had that conversation with Brad. I told him that for the past three months I'd been waiting for the text or the conversation where he would say, "You're not good enough for me."

I told him, "I've been living with that pain for the last three months."

He said, "I'm not going anywhere."

But my little girl was saying, "Don't believe him. Brad will find something terribly wrong and will take off, and I'll be left alone with more shame. I will feel so dirty."

I told him that I hadn't had many—or any—healthy relationships in my life, and this was probably the best I'd ever had. He was the healthiest man I'd ever met. He never pushed himself on me—never tried to hurry me. He let me initiate. I was the one who said, "I want a kiss."

Brad had his own coping mechanisms. He managed his feelings of rejection by being busy. He had what I referred to as a "Martha Stewart" gene. He couldn't bear even one speck of dust on his bike, so he'd polish it all the time. I joked that I would buy him a case of Pledge for Christmas. "It's beautiful that you take care of your things," I said. "But there's a point where that shouldn't be quite so big a deal."

Brad lived on ships. He knew where everything was. Every object had a place. His mother had nagged him to do things correctly, turning him into a bit of a perfectionist to guard against being verbally attacked or humiliated.

On the other hand, if you opened my closet door, it would look like a bomb went off. Drawers? I fold nothing. He never criticized me, but I had to let him know that this was one area where we were different. I was likely never going to change, even if I did my best to be organized.

I told him, "This is how I'm wired. If you expect me to meet you at your level of perfection, I'm going to fall short and I'm afraid you might use that against me—to hurt me or belittle me. And I won't be okay with that. And as for housework? I'd rather make money or exercise. This house won't get disgustingly dirty, but I'm not the girl who will spend four hours cleaning it from top to bottom. If I can afford it, I'll pay someone to do it. If I can't afford it, I won't do it. I'll piecemeal it."

Brad was clear too. "Okay! I've got it!"

We had our less than perfect moments. He had anxiety issues about being attacked for going to work. He had shame and fear about his value that was all wrapped up in serving others and giving to others. Even in our intimacy, he was not used to having his needs looked after. He was focused only on giving pleasure. Only once or twice in his life had he known pure pleasure just for him.

I wasn't having it. I had no intention of just taking from him. We were in this together and we would derive equal pleasure from our intimacy. While I wanted to be the best partner possible, I also had unresolved issues. A voice reminded me that if I had fun or joy, I would face punishment. If I let myself go, something bad would happen. That came to the surface quickly with Brad. So I was often scared and guarded.

I was open with him about my fears—that if I really let myself enjoy him, and our relationship were to end, it would devastate me. Before Brad, I had only had one man who I enjoyed sex with, and it had been like a drug. I was afraid of not being able to create that with Brad, and I was equally afraid that if we did create that and it fell apart, I would be crushed.

I knew I had to work on it. I turned to eye movement desensitization and reprocessing (EMDR), an integrative psychotherapy approach that has been extensively researched and proven effective in cases of post-traumatic stress. It also helps address shame, particularly body shame.

It worked, but I was still cautious because I had never felt safe around a man. I always felt that I would have to give myself away. Or I would have to beg for acceptance or beg for love. These were my wounds. So we took our time. But we also made a pact, knowing that our stuff would come up, knowing it would trigger each of us at some point. We agreed that there would be no "fuck-it" button. No one would run away and abandon the other.

I had to trust that he would not leave me.

One day, we went to Victoria, where we stayed at the Laurel Point Inn and visited the Oak Bay Rose Garden—my safe spot when I was a child. We posted a picture of us on Facebook. His old girlfriend posted, "I'm happy for you."

I looked at the girl and said, "Who's that? She's pretty."

"That's my old girlfriend," Brad said.

"What?"

He had three old girlfriends who were Facebook friends.

"That's awkward," I said. "And that's uncomfortable for me. Am I going to be your next old girlfriend?"

I shut down. My emotions were telling me, "This guy's a player and he's playing me and he will fuck right off and it will be another life lesson—the kind that tells me I should just be a nun."

My rational mind didn't play any part in this. I lashed out. "So, you fucked them too, right? And they're on your Facebook page—and now you have a picture of us on your page. I'm feeling pretty insignificant—like I'm not that important to you. I'm uncomfortable."

After that, my voice shut down. I couldn't talk. He waited. He sat with me. I breathed. He told me later that I was panting like a wounded animal.

I let the pain come over me and through me. Brad told me that at the time, all his instincts told him to run. But he didn't.

In the morning, he asked if we could talk it through. "This isn't about you not being there," I told him. "This is about my father not wanting me. Somebody else is more important. I have the evidence."

I also told him that I didn't have any old boyfriends on my Facebook feed. And they weren't cheering me on when there was a new man in my life. Brad explained that he and his girlfriend parted as friends—no bad feelings.

But I was jealous, insecure, and uncomfortable. I couldn't trust that he wouldn't toss me aside—that I wouldn't be just another old girlfriend. I apologized for my aggressive stance. It was none of my business how many women he'd been intimate with. We talked more and then had fun for the rest of that weekend. Still, I was disturbed by the amount of pain that raced through me—pain I couldn't stop. And try as I might, I could not reconcile his old girlfriend on his page commenting on us—no matter how *nice* it was. I thought it was strange and I didn't like it.

Through it all, we developed a little in-joke about running away: going to the store for a loaf of bread—and never coming back. If we were having a hard time, I'd look at him and say, "Are you going to the store for a loaf of bread now, Brad?"

But Brad committed to me. And I liked him a lot. Even my son said, "Mom, you like him a lot."

"He's the best man I've ever met," I said.

We made plans for the future. But when he was with me for his two weeks off, he started exhibiting tension. In the last few days before leaving, he'd run all over town, trying to do too much and getting stressed. At one point, I said, "I'd like to have some time with you. I want to be close and touch you before you leave."

I wasn't always available when he wanted to be with me because I worked all day. When I had time, he was either preparing for work or fixing stuff for other people. I said to him, "If you are rescuing other people at the expense of your own harmony, it's not okay."

He was angry with me for saying that. But just before he went back to Vancouver, I booked a date for us at Mahle House, my favourite restaurant. I was giving him what I wanted—some romance and an excuse to get dressed up.

But I was stressed. My guts were twisted in knots. He could sense that I was in an odd place, feeling rejected because I'd told him I wanted time with him, and he hadn't made that time. I felt unimportant—like I didn't count. My internal pain showed up as gut pains.

We had a lovely dinner and came home. He asked me to drive him to the airport the next morning. I agreed and set my alarm for 4.15 a.m. I crawled into bed, still in pain. I was tired, but I had a hard time sleeping. And he was next to me, not sleeping either. The room was full of tension. I finally drifted off and when I woke up, he wasn't there. He had gone to sleep on the couch.

The next time I woke, it was to the alarm. But Brad had left. I sent a text: "Where are you?"

"I thought I'd give you some space. I stayed at Don's and caught a taxi to the airport."

"You didn't even say goodbye to me."

"I didn't want to disturb you. You were sleeping."

"Brad—you'll be gone for two weeks. A hug and a kiss would have meant the world to me. You would have been saying goodbye to me like I count. I kept my end of the deal. You asked me to get up early to take you to the airport, and I woke up."

"Well—there was this tension."

"Yes—there was tension. Sometimes tension is there, but you did not keep your word to me. You didn't even tell me you were leaving. You left without saying goodbye. Don't ever do that again. That completely breaks trust with me. How am I supposed to trust you now?"

"I can't talk about it."

"Okay."

Brad's past was all about anger and tension in a relationship when he was getting ready to leave.

"You know, I don't have any history around you leaving," I said. "I don't have a history about you packing your bags and being angry with you. What you're telling me—that's your stuff—that's your wounding and now you're making me pay for it. I'm not that girl. I accepted that you're going. I would have appreciated it if you would have had enough consideration for me and my heart to kiss me and hug me and say, 'I'll figure out how to get to the airport myself.' That's what I wanted."

I went quiet after that.

It took a while for him to call me again, and when he did, I could hear the pain in his voice.

All I managed was, "Based on your behaviours, do you want out of the relationship?"

"Yes," he said. "I want out."

"Okay," I said. "Just let me know what you need. If you're planning to take your things when I'm away in Mexico, let me know. I want to be prepared. I wish you the best because you really are a lovely man."

There. I had all the validation I needed that I was not worth loving. I was not enough. But at least I had given myself permission to take a risk. I was proud of myself for that.

But before I could hang up, he said, "I really love you."

"Okay," I said.

"I don't want this to end."

My walls were already up, and I was putting extra mortar on those bricks. "Right."

"I want to work this out," he said.

"Sure. Whatever. You also asked me to drive you to the airport and then you fucked off on me."

We had no communication for the next couple of days. And then my son asked, "What happened, Mom? Why are you so sad?"

I told him what had happened with Brad.

Konrad shook his head. "Mom, he feels like he's not good enough for you. That's why he left. He thought he was disappointing you and that he would continue to disappoint you. He thought he wasn't worthy of you. You're both very broken. Men don't do well when they feel that they disappointed their girl. What men do when they think they're not good enough is that they throw themselves under the bus and leave. That's exactly what he did. Mom, you're a powerful woman; he'd have a hard time believing that he'd be enough for you."

I thought about those words. Because if that was true, which I believed it was, then he'd pack his bag and I would feel abandoned—that was the dance.

"Okay," I said. "I get it."

All along, I had prepared to be abandoned. I was ready to put on my armour and shrug and walk away. That was also the dance.

I waited another couple of days before calling him. "Can I have a clarifying conversation with you? What is it that you want? Are you going to come back and take your things and move on, or do you truly want to work on this with me?"

I heard his tears. "I really love you. I want to be with you."

They were beautiful words, but I still didn't trust him. "I'm willing to hit reset," I said. "I'm willing to talk, and I hope we never go through that experience again."

We talked about where he had dropped the ball and where I had made mistakes. When he told me that I got to be with him for two full weeks every month, I told him no. "That's bullshit. I work full time. I'm lucky if I see you on the weekend! I have needs. This is your delusion. This is the truth of it. All I want is affection. I want to be able to count on you and to trust you. If I can't trust you, we're done."

I was always waiting for him to leave. And that was my abandonment issue, because my dad never stayed. I was always waiting for the comment: "This isn't working for me. There's something wrong with you."

I expected him to discard me. Even when we were in Mexico on a carefree, relaxing vacation, I anticipated a *Dear John* letter. I told Brad that I had been carrying this burden, and then when he left on that night, my fears were validated.

Weeks later, we talked about it again. He explained that he'd tried to hug me that night, and I had pulled away. I didn't remember that at all. Was I almost asleep already? For him, it brought up all the rejection he'd experienced from his mother and his ex-wife. He felt discarded. Emotions and thoughts whirled through his head. He thought maybe he'd fall asleep on the couch, but images of abandonment wouldn't leave and wouldn't allow him to sleep. So he left, feeling wounded. It didn't occur to him then that I would feel abandoned when I woke up and found him gone.

CHAPTER 12

My father died in the early spring of 2019.

Days before his death, he phoned and left a voicemail message. He called repeatedly, each time leaving longer messages: as a child of three or four or five or six, I had been responsible for his pain, he lamented. I stopped listening to the messages. He called dozens of times a day, my phone buzzing like a nest of hornets.

I finally called back, and he rambled about pain in his knee. I couldn't help, I said. Perhaps his wife could do something?

He called again—and again—and again, each time saying, "I'm sorry. I'm sorry."

What was he sorry about? Did he have any idea what he had done? Did he know what a cruel and selfish man he had been? Did he understand what he had done to me, or was he trying to absolve himself and wash away his guilt?

I couldn't fully identify my feelings. Apathy? Perhaps I had a sense of relief that he would have to face his maker and confront his actions and, more to the point, his inactions. He hadn't been a father. He hadn't been honourable or kind, and he hadn't cared about me or my brother.

All he had cared about was victimizing us. Now he was playing the victim.

His wife called, crying, saying that he wouldn't stop calling me; he had lost his mind. I told her that my father was mentally unstable and had been for most of my life.

She had never seen him like this. She didn't know that he had been behaving this way for years—not just in the last few days. Nor was she aware that he would ignore me for months or years and then start phoning me, bullying me, hurting me, inviting me to see him and then cancelling at the last minute, saying that I wasn't welcome to come to his house even after I had gone to considerable expense and trouble to visit.

Finally, she called and said he was refusing food and I knew that he was ready to leave his body. I put a request on Facebook for my friends to pray that he would leave his body with ease. I sent my own prayer, saying, "I forgive you. I give you permission to leave your body. I will let go of my hurt and my rage. I will let go of my desire to hurt back."

Two hours later, he died. I was riding home on my motorcycle and could feel it viscerally: the moment he became an out-of-body spirit.

His wife called to tell me, and I was grateful—grateful that he had left his body and that he could no longer hurt me and terrorize me. I told his wife that she had been an angel to help him for so many years.

Today, Brad and I are together. We love each other. He is an integral part of my long-term vision. But deeply embedded in the back of my psyche is a doubt. I can't completely trust him. Not yet. Not today. Maybe and hopefully tomorrow.

Because of the trauma I experienced early in my life, I believe I have an attachment disorder. And if that sounds like an egregious self-diagnosis, I suspect if you've come this far, you're probably nodding and saying, "Yeah—that makes sense."

A dear friend of mine is a trauma therapist, and when I told her, "I think I have attachment disorder," she said, "How could you not? Nobody allowed you to feel secure and safe. If you didn't get that security as a child, you're not going to be able to form attachments properly as an adult. This is about slowly healing and building trust."

"Will I ever be able to heal this?" I asked her.

"With time," she said. "It will get better, but it's a process. It will take a few years."

I was so grateful to her. I needed to hear what she had to say because I also felt untrustworthy because I didn't know how to fit properly inside my skin or how to be a "normal" person—whatever that means.

Brad told me that he's scared too. He could go to work and come home and be told to leave because I had a new lover. That had happened to him. "But you're not like that," he said.

"No," I said. "I'm not that kind of person. That's not how I end a relationship. I'm usually willing to talk about issues and to go to a therapist. The reason people bond is to heal their unresolved childhood wounds—and we both have abandonment and betrayal issues from our childhoods."

His *Mister Martha Stewart* complex is still one of our issues.

I told him, "If you continue to constantly criticize me, it will be impossible for me not to fall out of love with you. You can't love someone who constantly picks on you."

"I'm so sorry," he said.

"The committee of assholes in my head is already so hard on me, beating me up regularly and telling me that I'm not good enough—I'm not smart enough—I'm too old—my life is over . . . that I don't need anyone else unleashing their committee of assholes on me. I'm doing a good enough job at making myself feel not good enough."

Brad looked at me for a minute and said, "Well, just so you know: my committee of assholes loves the shit out of you. I adore you. You're precious."

And I told him, "I know this is just about you following your childhood programming, and I try not to take it personally, but I can't accept you doing it regularly. How will I feel safe around you? I'm going to be like a cowering mouse running and hiding in a corner waiting for you to swat me with the broom of your words"

"I'm the one with the problem," he said.

"Yes, you are," I told him. "This is your problem, and I'm giving it back to you. I'm not letting you put it on me. When you tell me what I have to do in order to be more acceptable to you, how is that supposed to make me feel good about me?"

But he doesn't want to do it. He doesn't even know he's doing it—this is his programming.

Brad recently got his three-year cake, and his sponsor said to him, "Now that you've been sober for three years, I think it's time that you should write the steps."

I cheered. "When you do the steps," I said, "You stop doing damage around the people you love. You're forced to look at your ineffective coping mechanisms."

I see these mechanisms as survival traits. If you come from an abused childhood, you become an addict and you become co-dependent. It's not that you're a loser or a drug addict or a drunk—you're an adult child, and the way you numbed-out as a child was to eat, run away, or live in a fantasy world. As you grow up, you have different choices: alcohol, drugs, sex, buying things—all designed to avoid that committee of assholes that we all take with us. These are survival strategies to stop the pain.

When Brad is here with me, I notice I am more on edge because I'm waiting for the fight. I have to learn to feel confident that no fight is coming. My nervous system is still in fight-or-flight mode. And when he's gone, I'm happy because I don't have to think about anything other than what I will do that day. But I'm also sad and lonely because he's gone. It's an interesting cycle.

In my long-term vision, Brad and I get married and build a home together on a beautiful piece of property. I see us going to Mexico in the winter and riding our motorcycles together—having fun.

I still struggle with trusting and feeling safe. I still expect the worst, and I'm surprised when it doesn't show up. There is a part of me that still looks for my value and validation outside of myself. It's not a constant, but it still comes in waves—and that is the legacy of coming from a family lineage of persistent fear and distorted thinking.

As I do the work and understand myself more and see how I survived some of that horrific abuse and trauma, I'm amazed that I'm still okay. My parents could only do what they knew. They did what was what done to them. They were helpless. I was helpless. Life experience programmed me to do what I did. I have come to terms with the fact that I could not have turned out any differently. I'm grateful that I made it this far. If not for the recovery work, I would probably not have made it past age 26—or if I had, I'd be picking up welfare cheques and living in a beat-up old trailer with no teeth and a litter of children.

But for the grace of God, I was given some remarkable teachers—and through them and the work I did with them and on my own, I have hope, understanding, and courage.

I only hope that those are qualities I can pass on and nurture in others.

AFTERWORD

Between finishing this manuscript and sending it to press, some of my life strings unravelled. And while I would like to gather them all up and tie them in a pretty bow, the best I can do is a knot or two – maybe a couple still dangling, but tidied up.

I suspect that as long as I live, there will be loose ends kicking up dust behind me.

I'm okay with that. Loose ends are one result of living a rich, full life where I continue to learn and grow every day.

The first loose end is Brad. We are no longer together. It still hurts, but I'm proud of how I handled our parting and I understand what went wrong. I am not a victim. Brad did not do his twelve-step work. His sponsor told him: it's time to do the steps. Brad shied away. He told me that his debt stressed him out. He needed to work and pay it off. That was his priority.

My heart went out to him. "I'm willing to hold space for you," I said. "I'm willing to wait. I'll be that partner who'll support you in handling that part of your history. How long do you need to pay this debt?"

"Eight months."

"I'm willing to hold space for you for that long because I believe in us."

Brad poured himself into his work, but on his days off he rode his motorcycle to Kelowna to see his mother or to Terrace to visit his son. For the next four-and-a-half months, I rarely saw him. He had no time for me. He was no longer warm and engaged. If we talked, I was the one initiating contact.

"I want to see you," I said.

"I have to see my mother," he said. "It's too far to go over to Vancouver Island on the ferry."

I protested. "You're riding five hours to see your mother and eight hours to see your son. Please include me. Bring me into your life."

For my birthday, I booked three nights at the Pan Pacific Hotel in Vancouver. A treat and celebration! "Please come," I said. "I would love to see you, just for a night or two."

He did not ask for time off. Instead, he sent a "Happy Birthday" text.

Then there were two angry and toxic phone calls. The term we use in AA is "dry drunk." When you don't work on becoming a better person, you revert to the same habits and patterns you had as an addict. Brad was substituting work for his former addictions.

I had a couple of days to sit with that before he called to say he was coming to see me. "Brad, what's going on? You don't want to do this, do you?"

The pause on the end of the line lasted too long. And finally, "No."

He admitted that he'd wanted to wait until he was here to tell me in person that it was over.

"That's cruel," I told him. "Here I am, waiting for you, excited to see you, thinking you're coming home to me as my partner, and what you're really doing is coming to break it to me that you don't have any intention of keeping your word. When we were first together, you said that you wanted to be with me for the next thirty years. I believed you. I made a commitment to you. You did not commit to me."

He still had to come to the house to pick up his things. Fine. I would not stick around. I got on my motorcycle and rode off, but the engine started knocking a few blocks from home. Gingerly, I rode it back and there he was.

I told him, "I'm really worried for you."

"Stop analyzing me!" he said.

"No," I said. "Work is your new addiction. You don't have a personal life."

He paid no attention. I didn't really expect him to. As he left, he said we would still be friends. The next day he unfriended me on Facebook.

I could analyze him and our relationship for the next twenty pages, adding scholarly citations along the way. And why would I do that? To make me feel better?

There was only one important thing I could do at the end of this relationship: forgive him and forgive myself - and love myself and what I did: I stood in my power; I did not compromise my integrity. Neither Brad's behaviours, nor anyone's behaviours define my worth as a human being. I have learned, after all this time, how to love a man. I did everything to help Brad become the best man he could be. I supported him and nourished him without complaint.

We were destined to fail, and now that we have, I feel compassion for both of us. But I also have a sense of relief that I am no longer in that dance.

Brad was not the one, but I know that there will be a man who is willing and capable of receiving my love. I'm on pause. I'll know when I'm ready.

I want someone to ride with – someone to hang out with, play with, and travel with. I want marriage. I want a man in my life. I know how to be in a partnership now. That was the gift from this relationship. I didn't have that confidence previously.

Now I know that I know how to love a man. And that's partially because of my friend and coach, Lenore. She helped me through it. No one taught me how to love a man. My past taught me to fight with them. She helped me find my dignity and self-respect. For that, I am immensely grateful.

Tangled in my story since the beginning is a thread that belongs to my mother. She has been living with me now for over four years. She came because, as she grew older, there was nowhere else for her to go. I didn't want her, but I also could not have faced myself if I hadn't tried.

It hasn't been easy. I experienced pain and years of hostility, and I automatically fell into the trap of being a victim with her. At the same time, I had to feel safe in my own house.

Slowly, I learned to look at her through my heart's eyes. I had to learn to love her where she was, not in the place I wanted her to be. I had to stop myself from spinning down into a story about her. I also had to mirror back to her the feeling that she's okay.

Usually, I just made dinner for myself, but I began to cook for both of us so we could sit at the table and eat. Over time, I left the hurt and resentment behind and found compassion. I found the tears inside me – tears for both of us. And those tears are still there, softening my heart.

I've applied for subsidized housing for her, but she's here now, and one of my daily practices is to ask myself if I am coming from a place of love and gratitude. I have to forgive her and I have to forgive myself while she is with me in this life. Only then will the pain and toxicity melt away. The highest path I can take is to love and forgive – that is the only way for me not to slip into the story of being a victim.

As I come from this place of heart, I notice the energy between us softening. I also notice that I can see her and the tragedy of her life. She has mental illness issues and probably suffers from PTSD. How could she not?

I have learned to be kinder, and maybe that is why she is here with me. She is a human being, doing her best. My aim is to give her dignity as she moves through the rest of this life: dignity, peace, and love.

The last thread is one I believe I can tie up with a beautiful bow: Konrad.

My son went into treatment and has been clean for over two years. Thanks to The Last Door, a rehab centre, he has stepped up to become a strong, beautiful man. He has a girlfriend who he loves. When Brad didn't come for my birthday, Konrad was there.

He's grateful for the life he has now. And I'm grateful for him. We are friends. He shows up. He is my family. We have an honest, transparent, supportive relationship, something I never thought would be possible.

I prayed and cried for five years: "Please don't take my baby." My prayers were answered. He's looking after himself and educating himself and learning how to live his best life.

They say that we carry in us the trauma of the seven generations that come before us; that the pain, suffering, and dysfunction pass from generation to generation. What remains unspoken is that healing and love carries forward for seven generations. I'm not doing this work only for me: I am doing it for my son and his son and his child's children and on into the future. I want to pass on not my pain and trauma, but my love and forgiveness. I look at my son and I believe that the future has begun.

THANK YOU

Thanks to the people who have inspired me to love myself and believe in myself throughout my lifetime. Thanks to the earth-bound angels who gave me the courage to step forward and be my best version of myself, and who gave me tools that I use every day. Thank you to the forces that put the perfect people in my life who helped me dare to dream, and to believe that my highest purpose could be realized.

Without my son, Konrad, I would never have stretched myself to be a better parent than my own. Your life gave me a reason to be fearless as only a mother can be for her child.

Thank You to my teachers; I have had the privilege of coming under the influence of many souls who shone a light for me to find my way through the darkness and pain.

Oh Sensei Richard Kim
Hon Lee
Diana Cherry
Fatha Taylor
Deborah Soloway
Valerie Kuilboer
Lisa Kloss
Mia House Women's Treatment Centre
The Last Door Recovery society
Rene Robinson
Haven House Society Nanaimo
The Excellence Seminars
Mark Smith Family Tree Counselling
Brett Vinning
Lance Jager
Brad Scott
Goody Niosi

I am deeply grateful to you, Goody Niosi, for taking the time and energy to support me in writing and completing this book. Words can't describe how your generosity has given me faith, hope, courage, and, most importantly, closure on the scars of my past 53 years of life. Thank you from the bottom of my heart.

My divorce lawyer suggested that I write a book when I was in my thirties. I wasn't capable of facing my whole story.

Then my therapist, Mark Smith, insisted that this book be written to help others heal. I could not have done this on my own. The pain and the losses were too close to my heart; the material alone would have devastated me. I am so indebted to your grace, your support, and your compassion for my journey. If one person is helped by my story, we have saved one more person from the depths and despair of generational trauma and abuse.

And thank you to Simon Lindley for editing and making this book so much better because he viewed it through a critical lens.

GERMANA ROVINELLI

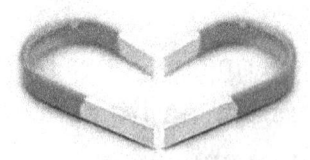

Attached.

THE NEW SCIENCE OF ADULT ATTACHMENT

AND HOW IT CAN HELP YOU FIND—

AND KEEP—LOVE

AMIR LEVINE, M.D. *and*
RACHEL S.F. HELLER, M.A.

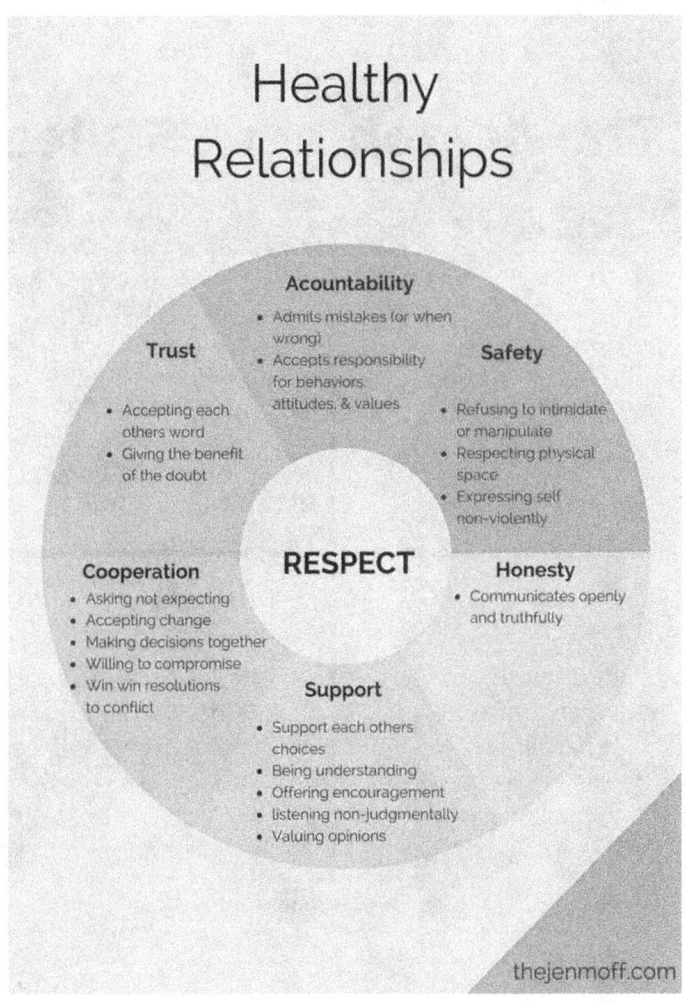

The Attachment Styles

SECURE
1- Can trust fairly easily
2- Is attuned to emotions
3- Can communicate upsets directly
4- Leads with cooperative and flexible behavior in relationships

ANXIOUS
1- Has a sensitive nervous system
2- Struggles communicating needs directly
3- Tends to "act out" when triggered (I.e. makes partner jealous)

AVOIDANT - DISMISSIVE
1- Downplays importance of relationships
2- Is usually extremely self-reliant
3- Can become more vulnerable when there is a big crisis

AVOIDANT - FEARFUL
1- More dependent in relationships than avoidant - dismissive
2- Strongly fears rejection
3- Has low self-esteem
4- Has high anxiety in relationships

@silvykhoucasian

WE DO RECOVER

FEARFUL AVOIDANT	DISMISSIVE AVOIDANT
Values intimate relationships more than dismissive avoidant	Tends to dismiss/block out connection in relationships
Experiences high anxiety in intimate relationships	Shuts down quickly when they become triggered
Fears rejection and has a low self esteem	Has an inflated sense of self and often judges others
Wants to depend on others and be vulnerable, but feels deeply fearful and distrustful	Does not typically depend on others, often career-driven and values self-reliance

Created by @silvykhoucasian
*Attachment theory by John Bowlby + Mary Ainsworth

GERMANA ROVINELLI

Securely Attached

~Focuses on creating "win-win" situations

~Is able to ask for repairs more directly from their partner

~Has strong self-soothing skills and is able to work though difficult moments

~Tends to be highly attuned and sensitive to their partner's emotions

~Is generally responsive/available when their partner expresses needs

~Has boundaries that are flexible and situation-specific

Created by @silvykhoucasian
*Attachment theory by John Bowlby + Mary Ainsworth

WE DO RECOVER

Dismissive Avoidant Attached

~Can appear very "well put together" and have an inflated sense of self

~Had to learn to rely on themselves for their own soothing and comfort

~Has difficulty being vulnerable and intimate

~Tends to dismiss "needs" in a relationship

~Can get in touch w/ emotions easier when there is a shared experience

~Tends to focus on others "flaws" as a way to maintain emotional distance

Created by @silvykhoucasian
*Attachment theory by John Bowlby + Mary Ainsworth

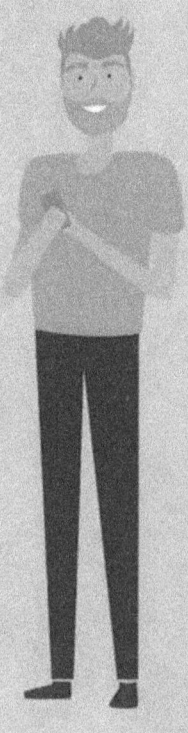

Anxiously Attached

~Sensitive to outside threats

~Strong fear of being abandoned

~Craves a lot of attention

~Wants a lot of closeness & intimacy

~Acts out when feels threatened

~Is incredibly giving and loving

~Struggles to communicate needs directly

Created by @silvykhoucasian
*Attachment theory by John Bowlby + Mary Ainsworth

WE DO RECOVER

Fearful Avoidant Attached

~Tends to feel used or exploited in relationships

~Can prematurely "pull away" from relationships when they feel rejected or overwhelmed

~Usually feels high anxiety when they begin to depend on someone

~Tends to crave emotional intimacy but feels deeply mistrustful of others

~Usually has a low self-image or some form of low self-esteem

~Has both "avoidant" and "anxious" tendencies

Created by @silvykhoucasian
*Attachment theory by John Bowlby + Mary Ainsworth + Mary Main

Avoidantly Attached

~Gets overwhelmed quickly

~Fears loss of self in relationship

~Feels easily shamed and exposed

~Can get in touch w/ emotions easier when there is a shared experience

~Has difficulty being vulnerable

~Dismisses "needs" in a relationship

~Tends to emotionally shut down during conflicts

Created by @silvykhoucasian
*Attachment theory by John Bowlby + Mary Ainsworth

WE DO RECOVER

Tools For Anxiously Attached

~Be willing to acknowledge your childhood pain

~Bring compassion to the parts of yourself that feel abandoned

~Question the validity of your fears when triggered

~Learn to express your needs directly

~Share your abandonment fears with those who earn your trust

~Work with a therapist/guide consistently to build a healthy relational template

~Learn to own when you project or act out on your fears in unhealthy ways

Created by @silvykhoucasian
*Attachment theory by John Bowlby + Mary Ainsworth

GERMANA ROVINELLI

Tools For Fearful Avoidant

~Be willing to acknowledge your childhood pain

~Bring compassion to the parts of yourself that feel used/exploited

~Learn to distinguish between those who want to use you vs. those who authentically give to you

~Set firm boundaries so you don't over-give and then become resentful

~Meditate/journal when you feel anxiety come up as you get close to someone

~Acknowledge whenever you act out or withdraw when you feel rejected

Created by @silvykhoucasian
*Attachment theory by John Bowlby + Mary Ainsworth

Tools For Dismissive Avoidant

~Be willing to acknowledge your childhood pain

~Bring compassion to the shut down parts of you

~Start paying attention to your subtle feelings

~Lean towards connection in small doses

~Learn to compromise in your relationships

~Practice sharing small vulnerabilities

~Learn to own/apologize when you dismiss others

Created by @silvykhoucasian
*Attachment theory by John Bowlby + Mary Ainsworth

ATTACHMENT STYLES

DISMISSIVE/AVOIDANT

TRAITS	TOOLS TO MANAGE
• High self-worth; finds it hard to trust others/partners	• Explore origins of low levels of trust for others
• Hypercritical about partner's emotional needs	• Become self-aware of hypercriticsm
• Will get close enough to be intimate but fears getting attached	• Be willing to feel into and confront the emotions that block intimacy
• Does not value attachments or bonds with others	• Explore how to create attachments while erecting flexible boundaries that ease as they become more comfortable with closeness
• Will only be intimate to the extent that it allows them to continually cycle closeness and distance with partner	
• Doesn't disclose much about themselves; closed off	• Be willing to become open and vulnerable

@LovingMeAfterWe

ATTACHMENT STYLES
FEARFUL/AVOIDANT

TRAITS
- Low self-worth; avoids getting close to partners due to high anxiety about feeling attached
- Fears rejection
- Wants intimacy/closeness but anxiety about this prevents them from following through and maintaining the attachment
- Typically unhappy due to anxiety about getting too close in relationships
- Won't reveal much about themselves in order to keep partners at arms length; Enough to get close but not attached

TOOLS TO MANAGE
- Needs validation around their fear of engulfment
- Needs a partner wiling to give space when overwhelmed
- Needs tools to ground themselves during high anxiety
- Seek understanding of their role in relationships which feeds their dissatisfaction
- Practice openness and reciprocal communication
- Learn to sit with anxiety and practice healthy relating with partner

@LovingMeAfterWe

ATTACHMENT STYLES

ANXIOUS/PREOCCUPIED

TRAITS
- Low self worth. Doesn't feel worthy of love; fears abandonment
- Hypervigilant about the relationship
- Craves closeness with partner
- Extreme highs and lows in relationships
- Unhappy with high anxiety and low responsiveness of partner
- Reactive around issues that threaten emotional security
- Feels capable about communicating with others about their own needs and wants

TOOLS TO MANAGE
- Must learn to self-soothe and regulate emotions during high anxiety
- Needs a partner willing to stay and process feelings during periods of high reactivity
- Must learn and practice personal boundaries and how to respect partner's emotional boundaries
- Needs to become aware of and heal relationship triggers to aid emotional regulation

@LovingMeAfterWe

ATTACHMENT STYLES

SECURE

TRAITS

- Strong sense of self-worth
- Sees others as worthy of love and trust
- Comfortable with love and intimacy
- High levels of confidence; vulnerability and commitment to relationship
- Good communicator, stable emotionality and remains present during periods of conflict
- Able to tolerate and process conflict with partner
- Maintains good emotional and physical boundaries

TOOLS TO MANAGE

- Needs partner who will check in on them to ensure their needs are being met in relationship
- Partner should be open to personal growth or risk losing them if relationship becomes too volatile or disconnected
- Should get to know their love language and path to co-commitment to increase self-actualization in and outside relationship

@LovingMeAfterWe

RECOVERY RESOURCES

12-STEP MEETINGS

All 12-step meetings are free to attend.
- Alcoholics Anonymous: https://www.aa.org/
- Narcotics Anonymous: https://www.na.org/
- Crystal-Meth Anonymous: https://crystalmeth.org/
- Co-dependents Anonymous: https://coda.org/
- Cocaine Anonymous: https://ca.org/
- Adult Children of Alcoholics and dysfunctional families: https://adultchildren.org/
- Al-anon: https://al-anon.org/
- Nar-anon: https://www.nar-anon.org/
- Overeaters Anonymous: https://oa.org/
- Sexaholics anonymous: https://www.sa.org/
- Gamblers Anonymous: https://www.gabc.ca/meetings

YOUTUBE VIDEOS

YouTube videos can help you understand abuse, trauma, the effects of unresolved repressed trauma, gaslighting, brainwashing, narcissistic abuse syndrome, signs of mental health issues, personality disorders, the effects of repressed trauma and abuse on our health, choices, and quality of life, and how to stop the cycle.

EFFECTS OF NARCISSISTIC ABUSE:

- Why You Can't have Healthy Normal Relationship (Codependency Recovery) | Lisa Romano
https://youtu.be/9KnjnSzx7WA
- Narcissistic Family Roles (Scapegoat, Golden Child, Invisible Child)
https://youtu.be/Rn3xhDni4w4
- 5 Signs Of Narcissistic Abuse (Parents, Friends, Co-workers..)
https://youtu.be/og8wA24x-dc
- The Body Keeps the Score: Brain, Mind, and Body in the Healing of Trauma
https://youtu.be/53RX2ESIqsM
- 3-Parts of the Narcissistic Relationship Cycle
https://youtu.be/Y1OGSeKsMlo
- The 4 Types of Narcissism You Need to Know
https://youtu.be/_uJs0iGQN0M
- The Shame People Feel When They Come From Narcissistic Families
https://youtu.be/nTyIOO6czJU
- How to Avoid Dating a Narcissist with Dr. Ramani
https://youtu.be/3ska9CXcuI8
- Ep 21: Dr Ramani Durvasula - How to Handle a Narcissist, Sociopath or Psychopath
https://youtu.be/j_GhsuXAlrc
- What is "love-bombing"?
(Glossary of Narcissistic Relationships)
https://youtu.be/WhILcuoVhgE

- The Best Explanation of Addiction I've Ever Heard – Dr. Gabor Maté
  https://www.youtube.com/watch?v=ys6TCO_olOc&feature=share&fbclid=IwAR0ENx8Nj-Npj8Zz2I5NFWaTn0id6XKPvcl_sG3JvKL0J9EM-jgBPYgNd48g
- Jordan Peterson - How to treat addiction effectively
  https://youtu.be/OyOnKZZ87mE
- 50 Symptoms of Narcissistic Abuse Syndrome
  https://youtu.be/VFhty3ruqKw
- Dr. Phil Talks About "Drop-Dead Deal Breakers" in Relationships
  https://youtu.be/b08AKE_8oDo
- The Psychopath & the Sociopath: A Masterclass
  https://youtu.be/gpjYtAB9i2w

COMPLICATED POST-TRAUMATIC STRESS DISORDER:

- What is C-PTSD? (Complex Post Traumatic Stress Disorder)
  https://youtu.be/NeQ8bgUAnFg
- How does being with a narcissist affect your body, mind, and soul?
  https://youtu.be/eJr1WQyNpH4
- Stephen Porges on the Link Between Feeling Safe and Making Change: PYP 340
  https://youtu.be/SvQrgf1SKeU
- Gabor Maté M.D - The Biology of Loss and Recovery
  https://youtu.be/17eS_1QNtdU

- When the Body Says No -- Caring for ourselves while caring for others. Dr. Gabor Maté
https://youtu.be/c6IL8WVyMMs
- Dr. Gabor Maté - Part 1 of 3 - Trauma and Recovery Across the Lifespan: Insight into Addictions
https://youtu.be/SGgwMe6y4hU
- Dr. Gabor Maté - Part 2 of 3 - Trauma and Recovery Across the Lifespan: Insight into Addictions
https://youtu.be/D5zDdiOFnV4
- Dr. Gabor Maté - Part 3 of 3 - Trauma and Recovery Across the Lifespan: Insight into Addictions
https://youtu.be/xwZsydIpe2U
- The Power of Addiction and The Addiction of Power: Gabor Maté at TEDxRio+20
https://youtu.be/66cYcSak6nE

RECOVERY SPEAKER LINKS FOR AA, ACA, ETC.

- Father Juniper AA ACOA ACA Inner Child Recovery
https://youtu.be/xthDyICrnhs
- The Secrets to a Healthy Relationship Explained| Dr. Nicole LePera & Lewis Howes
https://youtu.be/knVfc_B0W6E
- Good boundaries free you | Sarri Gilman | TEDxSnoIsleLibraries
https://youtu.be/rtsHUeKnkC8
- Jack Kornfield & Tara Brach: A Steady Heart in Times of Crisis | Guided Meditation
https://youtu.be/RqTD8TqIyjg

VITAL RESOURCES :

There's a lot of information in this link—also vital resources:
- https://find.healthlinkbc.ca/ResourceView2.aspx?org=53965&agencynum=17649917

And I want to note that it is best to go into a treatment centre that is *not* co-ed.
- The Last Door: Alcohol & Drug Addiction Treatment Program
  https://lastdoor.org/
- Westminster House: Women Do Recover
  https://www.westminsterhouse.ca/
- The Last Door: Youth Addiction Treatment Program
  https://lastdoor.org/addiction-treatment/youth-program/
- Aurora house: Partnering for Healing, Hope and Freedom
  http://www.aurorahouse.ca/
  (This is in a hospital and is an excellent women's treatment centre.)
- Broken Toys Broken Dreams
  By Terry Kellogg, M.A.
- Healing The Shame that Binds you
  The Family
  John Bradshaw
- For Your Own Good
  Banished Knowledge
  Alice Miller

- Taming Your Outer Child
  Susan Anderson
  The four Agreements
- Don Miguel Ruiz
  Dodging Energy Vampires
  Christine Northrup. M.D.

ABOUT THE AUTHOR

This book is about my Recovery journey from a family that taught me to sacrifice myself and die early, I did twice in early addiction to finding my way out of a personal HELL that I was set up to live as a family system of Don't Think Don't Talk Don't Feel. Don't be who you are because who you are is NOT GOOD ENOUGH. Seven generations of shame and secrets were programmed into me, as I found myself asking " how did I come to believe that I am worth so little," I was lead back to my family of origin and its hypnotic programming"

I have been in recovery for 29 years and my book is a reflection of my journey, painful transparent, and factual.

It teaches us that we are all Worth Loving.

This book is for: Personal development, Relapse prevention, treatment centers, second stage recovery.

Helping people who have been abused as children understand why they've been abusing, neglecting themselves, and how to stop this cycle of self-harm and self-abandonment.

Germana Rovinelli lives in Nanaimo BC

CPSIA information can be obtained
at www.ICGtesting.com
Printed in the USA
BVHW030433160221
599403BV00057B/101/J